Sewing

for Beginners

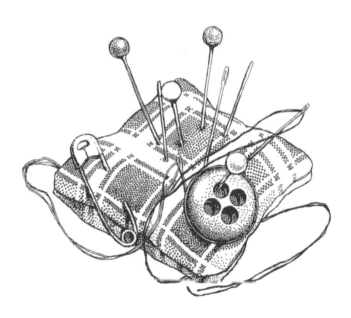

Printed in the United States of America.

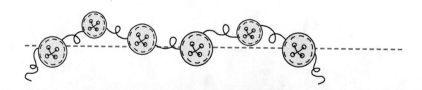

Table of Contents

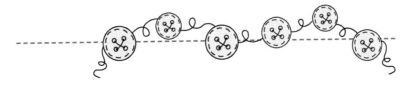

Introduction

Hi there!

My name is Diana Hansen, and I want to thank you for opening this book. I've been sewing just about all my life, and I've had some professional instruction and picked up some handy tips and tricks along the way. I really don't remember how old I was when I started sewing, but I know my grandma showed me how to make little crosses on a piece of fabric with different colored threads and I loved doing it.

I'm hoping that you'll go on to read this whole book and— most important to me and my ego—consider it a valuable handbook and a quick reference guide to making you look your best at all times, and your most professional when the occasion warrants it.

We're going to start by going all the way back to the beginning—when you get dressed in the morning. You know you look great when you've got on a brand new outfit and it fits well and looks crisp and neat. Don't we all? But what about when it's not new anymore? A button falls off, or you've snagged your pant leg on something that you just walked by—or you've washed and dried it and it just doesn't look the same. What do you do?

That's what I'm here to help you with. I want to tell you, and show you, how to make hand-sewing repairs on your clothes and how to keep your work clothes looking their best.

If you're like me, you've read quite a few books and seen plenty of internet websites and videos about hand sewing. I've seen explanations and pictures of different types of hand stitches and what the names of these stitches are—yet with very little instruction on how to make those stitches. I've read about which type of repair needs which stitch, what that stitching looks like when it's done, and sometimes a picture of the garment before and after the repair. I've even seen a video of a woman explaining and showing how to knot your thread (it was much more complicated than it needed to be, and it took her four or five times to get it right. I think I would have edited the botched tries out, but hey, that's just me.) If you go looking for material on the subject of business wardrobes, you'll mostly find discussions of what to wear with what to highlight your coloring, and what to buy to enhance your figure.

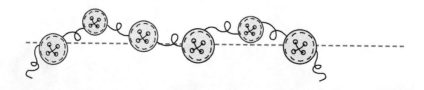

That's not what this book is about. I'm not going to try to tell you that you'd look better if you dressed for work according to my suggestions—or what colors go well together. I respect your intelligence, and I just want to share my knowledge of a useful set of skills that you may not have had the opportunity to learn before now, because frankly, it's hard to find information on this stuff out there on the information superhighway.

What I will be explaining and showing in this book is how to keep the clothes you already have looking good and in turn make yourself look good when you go to work. And I've also put in a few words about where you can buy good quality clothes for very little money, if you're interested.

So how is this book different? Well, I'm going to help you learn how to do the sewing from the beginning. I'm not just going to "teach" you different types of repair stitching and then show you a picture of the finished job. What I am going to do is come over to your house—in the format of this book, if I'm invited—and chat with you about a lot of things. Like why we need certain types of repair for different types of clothing damage —and how we do each of them. I'm also going to show you every step of the way in photos so you can do it with me, check your progress, and feel confident that you are learning a new skill—and learning it well.

When I explain the stitches, I'm also going to explain how to hold the fabric for ease of sewing, how to actually go about repairing a ripped sleeve, or hem a too-long pair of pants, etc.—and how the job looks in progress. There are a lot of pictures in this book, and most of them are simply photos of my hands doing whatever we are talking about so that you can look at the picture and compare it to what your hands look like doing the same thing. I want you to understand that you really can do this well, even if you've never tried hand sewing before. I'm going to tell you and show you in depth, every step of the way.

I would be very happy, too, if you discovered that sewing is a relaxing pastime for you, but that's not a requirement. My aim here is simply to help you learn how to keep your clothes looking good.

Thanks again for taking a look at my book. ***I hope you'll enjoy the time we spend together sewing!**

Diana

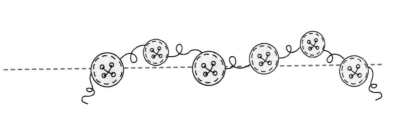

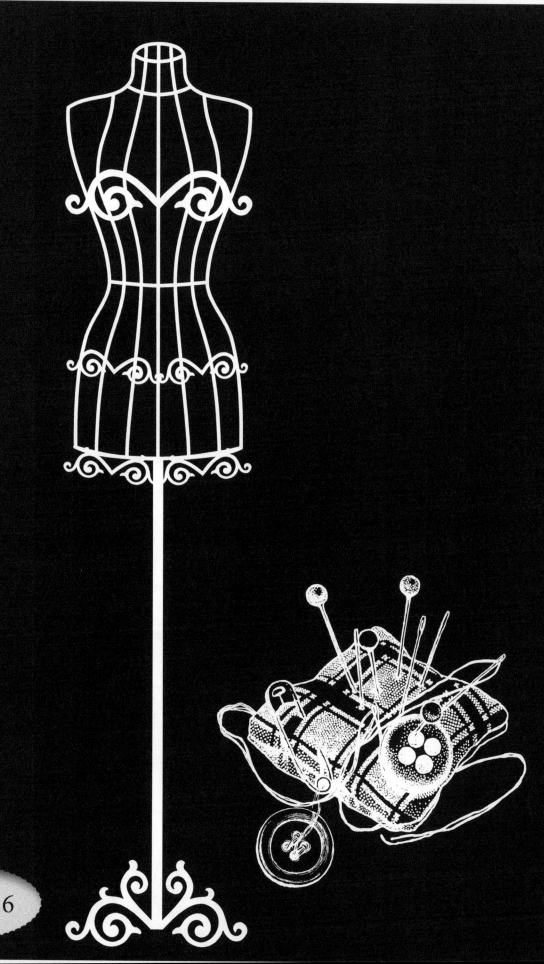

Yes, You CAN Learn to Sew!

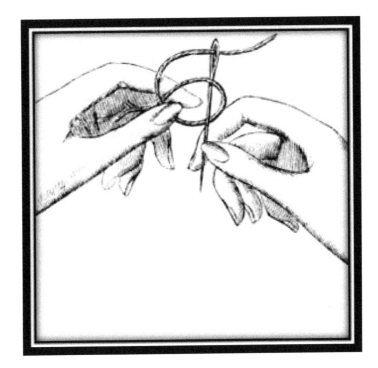

Yes, you can. Everyone reading this now might have a different reason why they think they can't, but I think most of those reasons will boil down to one, which all of us have uttered at some point: "I've never done this before!"

Listen up, you skeptics: I think that you can do something you've never tried before if you have a companion (in this case, me) who will tell you and show you how to do each part, and who will explain what any technical terms mean while still respecting your intelligence.

continued...

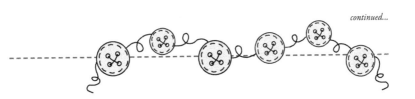

Author's Aside

One of my biggest pet peeves is when people have learned some technical thing and its accompanying jargon, and they try to impress others with their knowledge by using all the big words and technical talk they can. We all learn different things. Can you speak French? I can. Can you play the guitar or piano? Find and name the stars in the constellations? Cook a gourmet meal? Well, I can't do any of those things. Some of them I have no interest in, and others I would like to learn but never found a person who could or would teach me in the detailed, visual way I need to learn. The point is, no one has any right to be any kind of uppity to someone who doesn't know something that they do.

Hand sewing is probably one of the oldest human skills there is. Who do you think made the cave people's clothes? Sure, they threw some animal skins/furs over themselves to keep warm. But what happened when those skins flapped in the breeze and then fell off when they were running, or something ripped, and the cavemen and cavewomen were suddenly freezing and there was no new fur lying around? Well, someone thought of sharpening a bone, tying some stringy animal gut onto it, and doing what needed to be done.

Luckily, we're not cave people, so we don't have to use animal guts (unless you're into that sort of thing) but the concept hasn't changed. All you need to do is put some thread on a needle, stick it in and out of the cloth and then make a knot and bite it off. Voilà! Your (whatever) is sewed/hemmed/repaired!

However, if you want to prevent a batch of tangles in the thread, ensure the stitching is sturdy enough not to rip out right away, and make sure the whole job is somewhere between neat and unnoticeable, then I'll be here to guide you along each step of the way.

Did I say anyone can learn? Absolutely. Both men and women have been excellent tailors throughout the world's history, and hand sewing is a universal skill that anyone can learn. If you're a woman, man, boy or girl, you can learn to sew and do a good job of it. There's nothing unmanly (or un-womanly) about learning how to sew. I've read that the Scottish tartans were first proudly made by their warriors to identify their clans. Military recruits receive a sewing kit as part of their basic gear. And finally, absolutely all of the finest clothing designers and tailors have been both men and women.

Hand sewing is one of the earliest human skills. Starting with cavemen trying to protect themselves from cold and injury and evolving all the way to high-fashion design, the actual technique of hand sewing is the same: Two pieces of material/fabric with a needle and thread to attach them to each other.

Hand sewing is not just a skill that was needed in "the old days" to darn socks and patch holes. I don't know of anybody who darns socks anymore, but I do think that repairing something in a way that no one will notice is definitely an art as well as a valuable skill. I also do embroidery as a hobby, and to me that is definitely a creative art. Some of my pictures are beautiful (if I do say so myself) and some were "uncompleted attempts" (but never failures.) While our purpose here in this book is not to talk about creative needle art, I just want to point out that the equipment, the preparation, and the sewing skills are pretty much the same whether you are making your pant legs shorter or sewing a piece of needlework art that's worthy of your living room wall. Bonus!

So, why do I enjoy sitting down with a needle and thread to do a mundane job like hemming a pair of pants when I could take it to a tailor or use a sewing machine? Well, there are a few good reasons.

Let's consider taking hemming jobs to a tailor. Tailoring can be pretty expensive—possibly $5.00 to $10.00 per pant leg (or $3.00 to $5.00 per shirt sleeve), and tailors don't do simple hand-sewing jobs any better than I can do them myself. The only time I think I would really use a tailor would be in the case of a good piece of clothing (like a suit or special-occasion dress), that doesn't fit me just right.

TIP If you can't find a dress or suit that's exactly the right size go a little bit bigger. A good tailor should be able to do a superb job of altering clothing that's too loose to fit you perfectly, and it will look great on you. Unfortunately, there's not much a tailor can to do make something too small look bigger and well-fitting.

So what about a sewing machine? Why don't I just use a machine and get the job done in a few minutes instead of sitting there sewing for Lord knows how long to hem my pants? Actually, there are a few very good reasons. First of all, if you don't already have a sewing machine, they are expensive. They can cost hundreds of dollars, and a machine that can do embroidery can often be much more expensive. Along with many other items we purchase, the sewing machine with the cheapest price often ends up providing the most problems.

In comparison with a sewing machine, the equipment you will need for all your hand sewing will probably cost you around $20.00. If you buy a sewing machine you'll still need all the same equipment plus a few additions.

Using a sewing machine is also a whole different concept than hand sewing. You have to know a lot of extra things before you even get started. Things like bobbins and tensions, a certain pathway of machine-needle threading, and the correct way to place and move your fabric on the machine. In the time it would take to master the use of a sewing machine, you could have finished this book and hemmed all of your pants by hand. So can we agree that we don't want to consider sewing machines just yet? I thought so. If we want to make clothes "from scratch," or maybe sew a hem on a king-size sheet or blanket, then yes, maybe a sewing machine would be a good idea. But when we're just learning about sewing and doing a small repair job, let's not try to build a skyscraper from the top down. Machine sewing is a whole 'nother book.

 *We don't need (or even necessarily want) a sewing machine or a professional tailor for clothes hemming or basic repairs. We can keep our wardrobes in tip-top shape with simple and inexpensive hand-sewing.*

I also find hand sewing relaxing. There are many things people do to relax. Some of those things are actually tedious, like Sudoku, crossword puzzles, paint-by-numbers, gardening, etc. But when you work at those hobbies and you have to focus your attention on what you are doing, that other, free-floating part of your mind gets its "time in the sun", as it were. When I am sitting in a comfortable chair doing my hand sewing, I can solve all the major problems of the world, get my own and my children's lives in order, and decide what I'll do about my finances. Of course those great solutions don't automatically go into action, (actually, the majority of them never do) but just letting my mind touch on them while my hands are busy making those stitches leaves me feeling more relaxed and able to face life when I get up from that chair. I love that feeling, and I want to help you attain it too, in addition to a wardrobe full of non-tattered clothes that fit you well.

 *Hand sewing can be a very relaxing pastime or hobby.*

Don't think you need to read this whole book before you can get started on your sewing. Read through it a portion at a time and start small, before going on to read about all the next steps and possibly getting the feeling that it's all too much for you.

As we start the actual instructions, just remember that we are going to go in easy, understandable steps, and we're going to have pictures for reference.

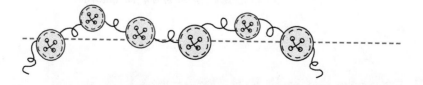

THE TAKEAWAY

► Hand sewing is one of the earliest human skills. Starting with cavemen trying to protect themselves from cold and injury and evolving all the way to high-fashion design, the actual technique of hand sewing is the same: Two pieces of material/fabric with a needle and thread to attach them to each other.

► In comparison with a sewing machine, the equipment you will need for all your hand sewing will probably cost you around $20.00. If you buy a sewing machine you'll still need all the same equipment plus a few additions.

► We don't need (or even necessarily want) a sewing machine or a professional tailor for clothes hemming or basic repairs. We can keep our wardrobes in tip-top shape with simple and inexpensive hand-sewing.

► Hand sewing can be a very relaxing pastime or hobby.

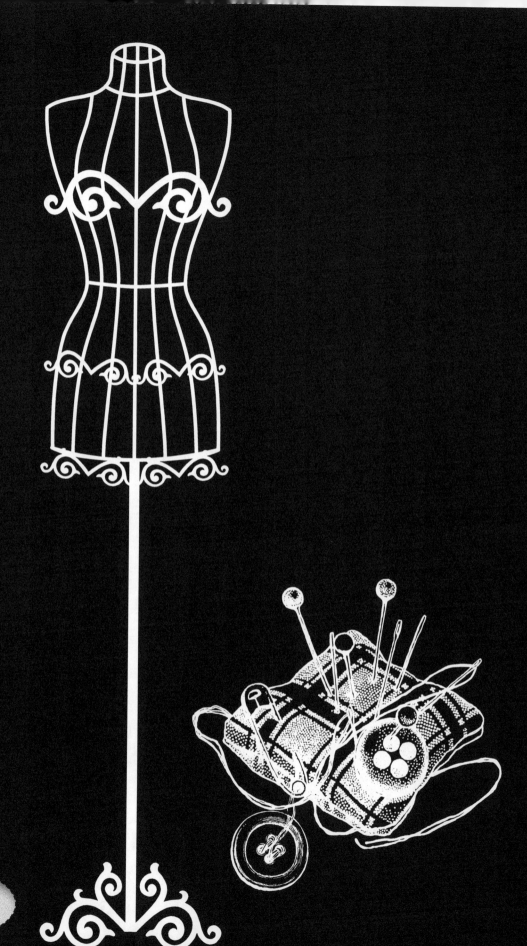

So Let's Get Started, Shall We?

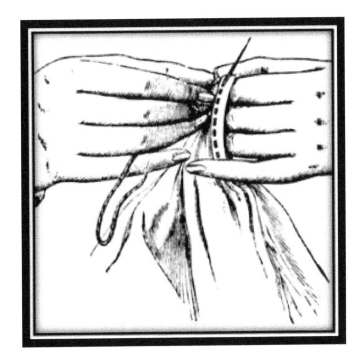

We are going to start with the basics, of course. You need to know the whys as well as the hows. If you don't understand why you need a hundred bags of concrete for your foundation, you won't know why your new house sank into the ground, and if you don't understand why you need to space your stitches evenly, you won't know why your finished hem looks awful.

What I'd like to give you in this book are two "baskets." The first one is your basket of knowledge, and the second is your basket of sewing equipment. These will serve you best when you keep all the parts together in a place that's easy to remember.

continued...

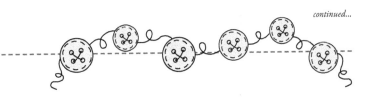

The Knowledge Basket

It looks exactly like this book (imagine that!) In it you will have all the instructions and pictures you'll need to complete your sewing projects. Keep it nearby and refer to it often.

The Sewing Basket

This is where you'll keep all your hand-sewing equipment together. It can look like and be whatever you want—a wicker picnic basket, a frilly hat box, or even a cardboard box with "Sewing" scrawled on the side with a marker. I use Christmas cookie tins.

 **KEY POINT** *By the end of this book you will have two baskets filled with wonderful things (knowledge and equipment) that will help you do quality hand sewing and keep you happy with a serene mind and nice clothes for years to come.*

Keeping it All Together

As with the knowledge basket, keep everything together in a convenient place. If you have or have had children, you will already have announced (many times) one of the basic rules of life: "If you put it back in the same place you got it from, you'll never lose it and you won't have to spend hours hunting around the house." If you haven't heard this rule before, you should learn it as soon as possible. It works very well in all phases of life— not just with sewing equipment (and especially with car keys, believe me.)

Equipment

*You don't need a lot of equipment to do hand sewing.
Your sewing basket should contain:*

- ▶ Needles
- ▶ Various Colors of Thread
- ▶ Tape Measure
- ▶ Box of Straight Pins
- ▶ Pin Cushion
- ▶ Scissors
- ▶ Seam Ripper
- ▶ Thimble and/or Pusher
- ▶ Buttons and a Container to Keep Them in

*You should also keep a little notepad and a pencil in there (not a pen
with possibly runny ink) to write little notes or measurements.*

When you've got all your equipment together, you'll need the basket or box you're going to keep it all in. These items are all relatively small and available at a low price, including the scissors. The store prices can range from inexpensive to ridiculous. You will get along fine with the low-priced version of each. You can get all of these items at Walmart, Jo-Ann Fabrics, or your local fabric store. In case you're just not near any of these, you can find plenty of these types of stores online.

*Okay. Now let's talk about the actual contents
of the sewing basket.*

Needles

Start with two packs of needles. Yes, packs. Don't panic: a pack has probably six or maybe eight needles in it. They usually cost about a dollar or two. There are packs of same-size needles, and there are variety packs. Get one pack of all same-size thin needles and the second pack should be all same-size thicker needles. Don't get a variety pack. They are quite useless because you won't have enough of the needles you need and will have some that you won't use at all.

Needles come in various thicknesses and eye sizes. (The eye is the hole where the thread goes through.) Base your choice of which needle to use on

continued...

the thickness of the cloth you are sewing. Thinner and finer fabric needs a thin needle so as not to make a noticeable trail of holes in it as you are sewing. It will also have a smaller eye because you will use a thinner thread. A thicker fabric (like denim) needs a thicker needle to push through the fabric, and a larger eye for the thicker thread. However, the needle won't leave noticeable holes in your project, because thicker fabric is denser.

There are many types of needles for many uses, but I usually use only "sharps" and "blunts" (AKA tapestry and embroidery) needles. Sharps are thin needles with a small eye for the thread to go through, and they're best for hemming or repair work on normal, fairly thin materials like cotton clothes, bed-sheet fabrics, etc. I use blunt needles for all my heavier sewing. Because the fabric is denser, you'll have to push the needle a little more forcefully to get it through, thus the blunter points so that you can feel the end of the needle with your fingertip—without putting a hole in your skin. This would be a perfect needle for hemming denim jeans, for example.

If you see needles that have the eye near the pointed end, they are sewing machine needles, so you don't need them. There are also "specialty needles" like the curved ones you often seen in the embroidery department—you don't need them either. There is no need for any kind of fancy-shaped needle except to make more money for the store. Just get two six-packs of regular needles—one thick and one thin.

Thread

You might be surprised to know that there are many, many colors of thread in every color of the rainbow. Keep in mind the color of the fabric you are going to sew when you buy thread. It just wouldn't be cool to sew a hem in a pair of black slacks with white thread.

There are also three basic kinds of regular hand-sewing thread that you can buy on small spools. These are light duty, dual duty, and heavy duty, and they cost about a dollar each. I usually have a mixture of dual duty and heavy duty thread on hand. I think the light-duty thread is very likely to break while you're sewing, and that is a real pain in the neck, so I rarely use it unless the fabric is so thin I can just about see through it.

In terms of thread colors for your sewing basket, a good start would be **black**, **white**, **tan or beige**, **red**, **blue**, and **green**. Thread is not very expensive, but you may not want to get all of those colors at once. If not, just get the black, white and tan, and you can always pick up other colors when you have a piece of clothing and you want to match well with the thread.

Tape Measure

It doesn't have to be six feet long, and it doesn't have to be expensive. I don't know exactly what they are made of—probably flexible plastic—but they are definitely not the metal snap-out ones you find in the hardware store! If you can easily bend the tape to measure something round, like your wrist or your arm, it's a good sewing tape measure.

Straight Pins

That's just what they are: small, straight, sharp-pointed pins with a little nub of a head on the top. They are used to stick into two pieces of fabric to hold them together while you are sewing. Because they have that little head, they are then easy to remove after you've stitched the area. I'd say they are about a dollar or so for a little plastic pack.

Pin Cushion

This is something that you can stick your straight pins in when you are not using them. The average pin cushion is red and looks like a tomato with a string attached with a little strawberry on the string. And, like much of our other equipment it's quite inexpensive—a dollar or two.

Author's Aside

I had no idea why they would think of pairing up a strawberry and tomato, but it turns out that the little strawberry is a fabric-colored emery cone used to sharpen your pins and needles. Huh? My pins and needles don't get dull. I leave them in the pin cushion when I'm not using them and they stay sharp. Well, maybe if you left them out in the rain, but…who knows? I still don't know why it looks like a strawberry attached to a tomato.

Scissors

You can buy scissors for a lot of money, a little money, or anywhere in between. Of course you get what you pay for, mostly in how long the blades stay sharp. You can use the cheaper scissors for hand sewing. Mostly all you need them for is cutting thread. They'll last practically forever. To tell you the truth, my hand sewing scissors are the small, curved baby fingernail scissors I've had since my children were infants. Maybe since they are curved, I'm not tempted to use them for cutting anything else (like paper) so they stay good. My oldest son is almost 50 now (geez!), so I can attest to the fact that the baby scissors really last.

Seam Ripper

A seam ripper is a very handy item to have. It is basically a small, J-shaped hook on a short handle. The idea is to carefully stick the longer side of the J under a piece of thread you want to remove and lift it up. The sharp edge of the hook will cut the thread, and thus rip it out without catching the fabric along with the thread. Obviously, you can do the same with your scissors, but it's a lot easier (and safer for your fabric) with the ripper.

Thimble and/or Pusher

Both of these items are used for basically the same purpose. A thimble is made to protect your finger(s) from needle holes, and you can also use it as an aid to pushing your needle through a very heavy fabric. For me though, a thimble is usually too small and always uncomfortable to keep onto any finger I try to put it on, and consequently it tends to fall off when I'm attempting to use it.

Instead, I have invented something spectacular that I call a "pusher." I could probably have called it something fancier that sounds more like sewing equipment, and I'll bet I could probably patent it too, but it's so plain and so easy to make that I'd probably never sell any, so I'm giving away my secret: Save an empty spool of thread. Then, find a Phillips head screw (the one with the cross slot on the head) that fits pretty snugly into your thread spool hole and is not quite as long as the spool. Screw it down tight with a screwdriver, and there you have a perfectly useful palm-of-the hand "pusher" that will get a needle through any kind of fabric. Just remember that the screw needs to be a little shorter than the spool. If it's longer than the spool, the pointy end will stick out into the palm of your hand—ouch!

Author's Aside

I'm sure you will have noticed my various mentions of poking holes in your fingers with your needle. But don't worry. If you take my stitching advice and get some practice, I'll bet you won't get any holes in your fingers more than once a year or so.

I came up with the idea of the pusher when I was trying to sew some Velcro onto a pair of Carharts (heavy denim work clothes) for one of my sons. It worked for that, so it will work for anything!

Author's Aside

My son is in the Merchant Marines. He does the sewing, splicing, tying, and cutting that all sailors have to learn. He has something cool that he showed me: It's a round piece of fairly heavy leather with loops around the edges of it, called a Sewing Palm. You loop the loops around your fingers, which holds the leather against the palm of the hand and, there you have the same functionality as our pusher. I think it would be much harder to make than our pusher—and if you bought one from Amazon.com it would cost about $20.00. I think I'll stick to the pusher. How about you?

Buttons and a Container

Let me explain one of the rules of life, if you don't already know it. Buttons are like clothes hangers. When you need one, you can't find one anywhere. Then you might go out and buy a couple, and sure enough everywhere you turn in the house, there are clothes hangers. It's the same with buttons, except buttons are a lot easier to keep track of because they don't hide in the back of the closets with two of them working together to hold up one shirt.

If you do hand sewing, inevitably you will find you have some extra buttons here and there. Sometimes you'll need one but you see some in the store on a card that holds four or six buttons, or sometimes you are discarding something or changing the buttons because you couldn't find one to match what's on there—and that/those button(s) are so pretty or unusual (or whatever) that you don't want to throw them away. So just find any kind of container that can be closed securely—a jar, (emptied and cleaned of course) with cover, maybe an empty cookie tin (I amass a lot of those!) etc. Pretty much anything will do. If you keep all your extra buttons in this container and in or with your sewing basket you'll always have buttons to look through for the one you want.

Notepad and Pencil

This could be any kind of pad or small notebook. You won't be writing a lot in it. And please, use a pencil. We don't want to stick a pen in with our sewing equipment, just in case the ink decides to leak. That could ruin our equipment and would be a messy clean-up job.

A Box for All Your Sewing Equipment

This is an easy one. Keep your sewing supplies in any container that is clean. It could be anything from a cardboard box to a plastic bag. Just make sure you label it so that you don't mistake it for garbage and throw it out.

Two More Things

I didn't want to scare you at the beginning, but you really should have an ironing board and an iron. If you want to have your hems and seams look like they've been professionally tailored you need to iron the creases. Also, you really should try to learn how to iron shirts and pants for when you don't want to look wrinkly (like at work), but we can talk about that later. An iron should only cost about $15.00—$20.00 tops, and the ironing board about the same.

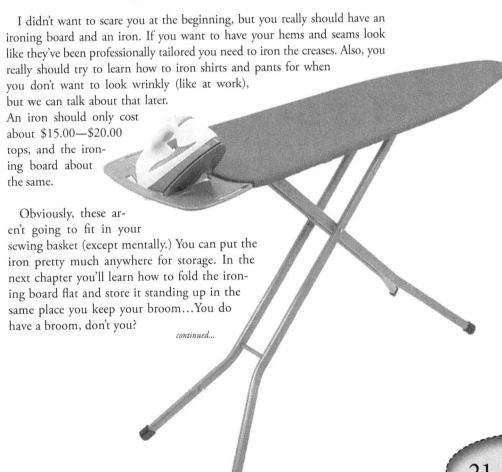

Obviously, these aren't going to fit in your sewing basket (except mentally.) You can put the iron pretty much anywhere for storage. In the next chapter you'll learn how to fold the ironing board flat and store it standing up in the same place you keep your broom...You do have a broom, don't you?

continued...

The equipment you'll need to do a thorough and neat hand-sewing project consists of the following:
- *Needles*
- *Thread*
- *Tape Measure*
- *Straight Pins*
- *Pin Cushion*
- *Scissors*
- *Seam Ripper*
- *Thimble and/or Pusher*
- *Buttons and a Container to keep them in*
- *Notepad and pencil*
- *Container for all your sewing equipment*
- *Iron and ironing board, stored separately.*

Please don't let this list of items upset or overwhelm you. They're all small and very inexpensive (except for the iron and ironing board) and they are all very useful and very easy to get the hang of (including the iron and ironing board.) We both know it's kind of a pain to buy all this stuff and get it all organized before you even get to do any sewing. But once you've started hemming a pair of pants or sewing on a button, the reward of having everything you need right at hand becomes obvious.

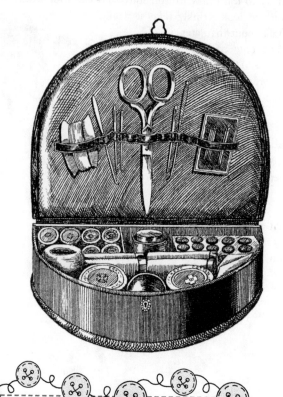

THE TAKEAWAY

▶ By the end of this book you will have two baskets filled with wonderful things (knowledge and equipment) that will help you do quality hand sewing and keep you happy with a serene mind and nice clothes for years to come.

▶ The equipment you'll need to do a thorough and neat hand-sewing project consists of the following:

- ◆ Needles
- ◆ Thread
- ◆ Tape Measure
- ◆ Straight Pins
- ◆ Pin Cushion
- ◆ Scissors
- ◆ Seam Ripper
- ◆ Thimble and/or Pusher
- ◆ Buttons and a Container to keep them in
- ◆ Notepad and pencil
- ◆ Container for all your sewing equipment
- ◆ Iron and ironing board, stored separately.

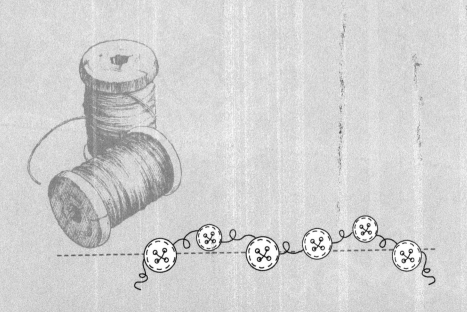

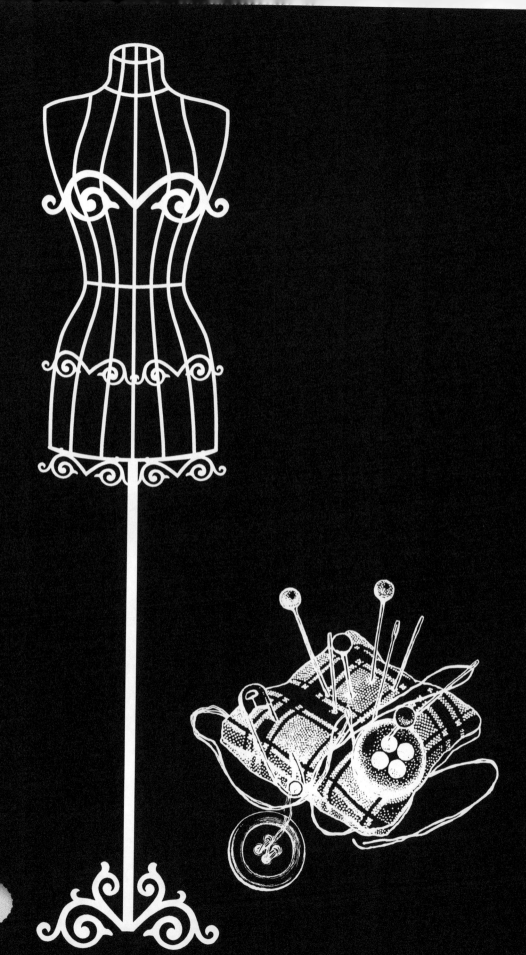

Ironing is the First Part of Sewing. I'm Sorry.

I **like to iron**. I'm probably nutty in that respect (Mom always said I was.) Back when I used to work, I'd put my phone headset on and call my Mom while ironing all my clothes for the week at one time. Multitasking!

Anyway, no matter how much you want to protest, you really need to do some ironing as part of the set-up for your sewing project. It makes the difference between your hem (or repair work) being so neat as to be undetectable, and your hem (or repair work) making you want to throw the item In the back corner of your closet and never look at it again, let alone wear it.

continued...

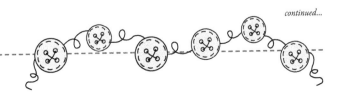

When starting any new job or hobby, you have to learn how to set things up properly before you get into it. You also need to pack things away properly when you're finished with each session. There's no other way to end up with a good job.

The first thing you need to do for ninety-nine percent of your sewing projects is set up your ironing board and iron. The way you got the ironing board from the store is the way it should be stored—folded with the legs flat, and the whole thing leaned up against a wall—preferably a closet wall and not your living-room wall.

If the fabric is very wrinkled, you'll benefit from ironing it before you sew it.

So let's plunge into this, shall we? Hold the ironing board upright so it's standing on its lower leg, pointy side up, and give it a hug. No, really. Put one arm around it across the upper leg, and with the other arm feel along the outer edge of what will be the underside of the opened ironing board. You'll find a lever there that, when you press it all the way into the underside of the board, will release the clip that holds the legs folded. When you've done that, you'll realize why I told you to give that board a hug. Your hugging arm will keep the legs from flopping out and possibly hitting you in the head.

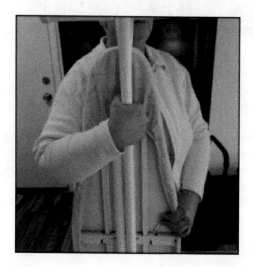

Here's yours truly, giving my favorite ironing board a hug (nah, I'm not a fanatic. I only have one ironing board.)

My perfectly set-up ironing board, ready to do its job!

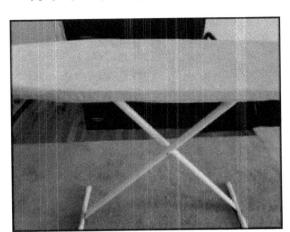

As the ironing board legs open within your gently restraining arm, you'll turn the ironing board so that the board part goes flat and both of the legs are down on the floor. The same lever you used to open the ironing board will also let you adjust its surface height. If you push it in just about half-way, you can move the board height up or down. As you (gently) release the lever, it will stay at the height you have it at that time. Most people feel comfortable with the board part at about bellybutton level.

When you're finished ironing (and you will get finished) you will close the ironing board just the opposite of how you opened it. Set it sideways so the back of the board (the flat end) is down and the lower leg is on the floor. Push the lever all the way in, and lift the top leg up so it goes flat against the underside of the board toward the pointy end. Give it the old hug-hold while you are releasing the lever and, voila, the ironing board is ready for storage again. Oh, and before you do this, make sure you've taken the iron off the board so it doesn't fall on the floor.

Author's Aside

I don't think I've ever in my life seen or used an ironing board that doesn't make some kind of wailing screech when you open and close it. If it doesn't when it's new, it will probably start fairly shortly. When you hear it, don't think you've bought a defective ironing board.

Okay, now for the iron. The first thing you'll do is fill the iron with water through a small opening somewhere on the top near the pointy end. Isn't it a lucky coincidence that both the ironing board and the iron have a flat end and a pointy end so we know which end we're talking about?

Set the iron on its flat end when you add the water. The iron's instructions might tell you to use distilled (or filtered) water, and of course that would be optimal, but if the water comes out of your faucet clear and not foul smelling, then it's okay to use it in the iron, as long as you empty it between uses. Yes, there might be some minerals in the water that could clog the iron, and the instructions may say tap water might make it not last as long. But at $15 to $20 for an iron, the difference between ten years and twelve years of use isn't much.

 Irons are one of those appliances that never seems to wear out. They are in much more danger of being left behind if you move than anything else.

Near the front end of the handle (by the pointy end) you'll see a hole. That's where you put in the COLD water that will make the steam that will de-wrinkle your fabric. There are two ways to fill an iron with water. SLOWLY from a measuring cup, or SLOWLY from the water faucet. If you go too fast the water will fill up the top of the hole, not letting any air escape from the hole and consequently not letting the water get into the hole. (It's the same principle as sticking a knife into a new bottle of ketchup, I think.)

So. You take the water-filled iron and put it on your ironing board, sitting up on its back (flat) end. Plug the cord into an outlet that is close enough so that your cord will be loose and you can move the iron around enough to do the actual ironing.

Now check the heat dial that should be near the handle. I keep mine set on "steam" and never move it unless I'm ironing some fabric so thin that I can almost see through it. I never bother turning it off either, because once you unplug it when you are finished ironing, it will cool itself off in a few minutes. So keeping it on the "steam" setting should be sufficient for just about all your ironing needs (like it is for mine.)

WARNING! Any time you leave your ironing board, even if only for a minute or two, UNPLUG the iron and put the plug end of the cord up on top of the ironing board with none of the cord hanging off. This is for the safety of not leaving something hot plugged into the electricity, and also for the safety of both parties in any possible dog, cat, or human or chair leg encounter with the hot iron's cord. The irons nowadays heat up in a few seconds, so you won't have to wait long to get started again when you come back and re-plug. Please do this. Better safe than sorry. Way better.

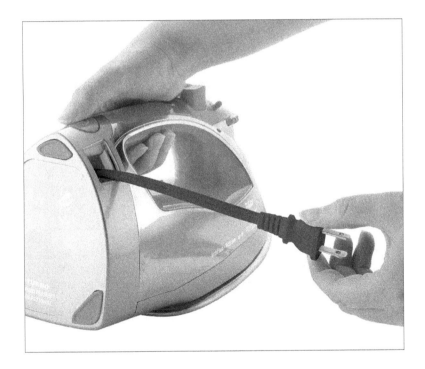

When you have finished your ironing session, put the unplugged iron on a heat-safe surface until it cools off. When it is cool, pour the water out of it. This will keep any minerals from hardening inside the water hole. Then put the iron away in its designated place in a closet somewhere. Don't be lazy and leave it out in the kitchen or living room. While you're at it, put the ironing board away as explained above. You might not use it again for a month, and as with the iron, it would look pretty tacky if you just left it leaning up against your bedroom or living-room wall all that time.

Hey, we're getting there. You've got the iron hot and ready to steam and the ironing board is standing there waiting to be ironed on.

The proper position of the ironing board and the iron is with both flat ends to your left, for a left hander, and to your right, for a right hander.

Now get your fabric. If it's very wrinkled (as you'll see mine is) you'll want to iron it flat before you can do any reasonable sewing with it.

Here's our wrinkly fabric. We don't like it.

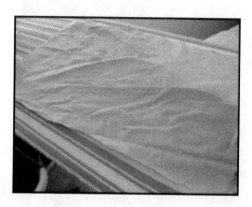

Just spread your fabric onto the middle of the ironing board in front of you. If the fabric is quite large, say a tablecloth or a curtain panel, there are a few tricks to controlling it on the ironing board, and we'll discuss them in a later chapter.

You don't always have to iron your whole fabric before you sew. If you can hold the part you're going to sew flat between your fingers, it's okay. If it's creased and lumpy between your fingers, you'll have a hard time sewing on it, so that's the time to iron it first.

Now, we're ready to iron! Let me tell you first of all that there are two ways you can tell if the iron is ready. One is to lower it down flat on the ironing board (not on your fabric) and see and hear if the steam comes out. If it does, you're good to go. If not, wait a little more. The other way is the good, old-fashioned way my mother taught me. Lick the tip of your pointer finger and give the bottom of the iron one (very) light, (very) fast tap with your damp finger. You'll hear a little sizzle if it's ready. If you don't hear it, it's not. You honestly won't feel this if you are quick and light enough with your finger-tapping. Some of the things I tell you to do might seem weird or old fashioned, but hey—I'm an old lady, after all. I'm telling you the way I was taught, and I find it almost always still works the best.

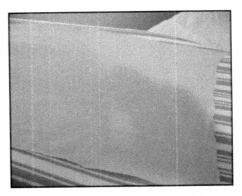

You smooth the fabric by moving the iron back and forth on the area you want wrinkle-free. If you stop for any reason, take the iron off the fabric and set it on its back end, off the fabric. Don't let the iron sit on the fabric for any amount of time without moving it. No amount of time. None. Did you ever see a shirt

Now the fabric is ironed. Beautiful!

with the outline of the iron on it in brown? (Hopefully this was in a cartoon of some kind.) That happens when you don't follow this rule. Even if you don't get the iron outline, you can still get those brown marks on the fabric and they don't come out. It's called scorch.

That's all there is to the art of ironing. When you get fancy and iron shirts or pants, there are a few other techniques to learn, but that's for later on. For now we just want to make the fabric wrinkle free and iron some creases on it.

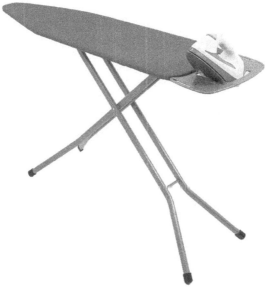

Author's Aside

I'm telling you EVERYTHING here so as you go along if you skip a step you'll know it. Sometimes you'll regret that skip and have to go back and redo it. Other times, you will be developing little shortcuts as you get better at hand sewing. For example, in the discussion above about ironing the fabric before you sew, you really only need to iron the edges where you are going to sew, if it's large. You'll do the "finish" ironing later.

And now for the pre-stitching preparation. (Huh?) I heard you. Now stop it. If you want to do this you have to do it right (I can feel my Mommishness popping out here.) You'll never get it to look decent if you don't do the setting up properly. I said sewing is relaxing. It is. We just didn't get to that part yet.

Before you start your actual stitching, you have to get your fabric or piece of clothing organized for the project. But don't forget, in this section we are going to use a plain piece of smooth fabric, like an old piece of sheet or a pillow case, or just a cotton rag or a handkerchief. We're going to sew it like the edge of a blanket (or napkin) so that it has a "finished edge" (folded over and neatly stitched) instead of a "raw edge" (not folded and the edge of the fabric all raw.) Just make sure the fabric is smooth and doesn't have tufts (bumps) in it. You will be able to sew over bumpy fabric later if you want to, but not yet.

First, fold over the edge of the fabric toward the inside. That means that the two inside (usually lighter in color or not as smooth) edges are together in the inside of your fold and the two outer edges are—you guessed it—on the outside!

You'll need to figure out how much of a finished edge you want to have on your fabric. I mean, if you had a pair of pants you needed to shorten by two inches, you would fold it so the edge is two inches wide, right? (Yes, we'll go into this in more detail in the hemming chapter, don't worry.) For our purpose of practice on this small piece of fabric you can make your fold any width you want, but not very wide—probably a little less than an inch. And please keep in mind that for practice we're using an eyeball measurement. When you are hemming or repairing clothes, you ALWAYS use a measuring tape to be exact.

As you fold up that edge, iron it so that you have a pronounced crease there. Be sure to keep the fabric flat so you don't get any extra creases that you don't want.

TIP A fold (as in "fold over the edge") is a gentle laying of one side of the fabric on top of the other. A crease is a fold that has been pressed down to the point that it looks sharp and flat and the mark of it remains when you open the fabric again. With a piece of paper, you might crease the fold with the edge of a ruler or something heavy while holding it flat. When ironing, you crease the fold with the heat, steam, and weight of the iron. (You'll notice sometimes it's referred to as "pressing" clothes or fabric, instead of "ironing." So now you know where that came from.)

At the upper edge of the fold, tuck in the raw edge of the fabric and iron that into a smooth crease.

When you've got that fold completed and ironed to a flat crease, then you fold a little flap of the edge of the fabric under again, tucking it into the first fold. Fold the edge about two inches along parallel to the first fold. Hold the fabric down against the ironing board with your thumb and middle finger (holding your index finger up and out of the way, carefully, —very carefully—put just the point of the iron on that fold between your fingers. You won't burn yourself if you just put the point of the iron there and wiggle it a little bit. Don't actually move the iron forward, or it will get too close to your fingers. When you've got that little spot ironed, then you can get your fingers out of harm's way and iron it a little better. Just that amount that you had folded between your fingers.

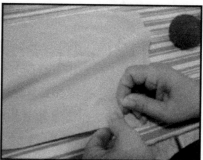

As you're folding and creasing, push pins into the fabric about ½ inches apart cross-ways to the fold, with the head of the pin toward the top of the fold.

As a result of this second folding and creasing, you will be creating a flap that is folded at both the top and bottom edges. As you're going along with this folding and creasing, you will also be sticking a straight pin crossways to the folded edge, about every inch and a half or so apart. Put the pin in so that the little nubby head is at the top part of the fold. That will make it easier to pull it out with your dominant hand as you go along when you are actually sewing the fabric.

And there you are! Just make sure you remember your safety tips about the hot iron, and you are all ready to sew the hem or rip or whatever you imagine your practice fabric represents (that is, whatever you plan to repair when you're done with this book!)

TIP I admit this preparation is kind of a pain in the neck, but you will see that the nice, sharp, folded and pinned sewing edge really pays off when you are doing the actual stitching.

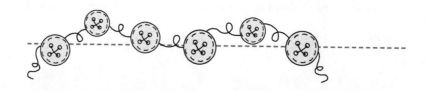

Chapter 3

THE TAKEAWAY

Let's briefly go over the key points in this chapter:

▶ When starting any new job or hobby, you have to learn how to set things up properly before you get into it (and put them away properly when you're done!) There's no other way to end up with a good job.

▶ If the fabric is very wrinkled, you'll benefit from ironing it before you sew it.

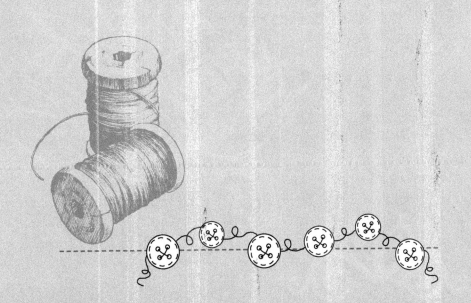

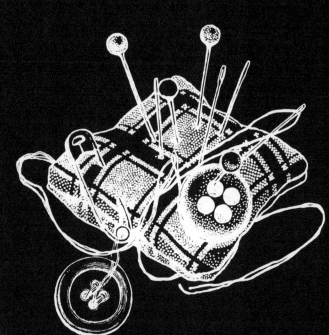

Let's Sew a Fine Seam.

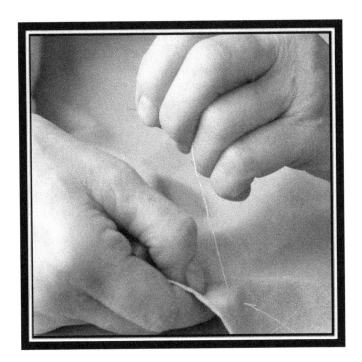

Wasn't that one of the old-fashioned requirements for a woman to be considered a valuable bridal prospect? Well, forget it. Times have changed. Quite a few men do their own sewing these days and quite a few women have no clue how to sew anything, so we're on an even playing field here. The only real requirements for high-quality hand sewing are reasonably steady hands, some patience (okay, maybe a lot of patience), and the ability to recognize a straight line.

I am going to spend some time here explaining and showing you exactly how to make a straight line of even, neat seam stitches. Once you get the hang of sewing a neat line of stitching, that's basically it. You're there! A line of neat stitches is the whole basic technique of all hand sewing. When you get that down pat you can sew pretty much anything (with my help, of course.) So now we're ready for actual stitching!

continued...

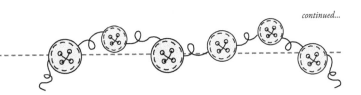

Shop Talk...

Seam stitch, noun. This is a straight line of stitching that you would use to attach two or more layers of fabric together.

The first step in stitching (or sewing) is that we have to thread the needle. This is not hard as long as you can see properly. If you need reading glasses, wear them for your sewing. If you're in your favorite chair, make sure you've got a good, bright light coming over one of your shoulders. (You'll figure out which side is best for you as you're setting things up.) I have a very bright light in the corner of my living room next to my sofa. Nobody likes it because it's so bright, so I only turn it on when I'm sewing. At other times we use one of the other, softer lights in the room.

The amount of thread you take off the spool to sew with is pretty important. Of course you don't want it to be too short, or you'll be stopping to tie off the end and rethread the needle every couple of minutes. But you don't want it to be too long either (thinking you'll be saving yourself some re-threading work.) Too-long thread inevitably leads to knots. Seriously. I've been sewing since I was a little kid, and every once in a while I make the thread too long. Then it tangles and I get a knot. I have to say a few bad words, cut off the thread below the knot, fairly close to the sewn fabric, and tie it off (make a knot) at the edge of where it comes out of the material, (on the inside, of course!) Then I have to cut off the thread above the knot (wasting the in-between thread), re-thread it, make a new starting knot on the inside, and go on from there.

Special Feature

"Stitching or Sewing?"

You might notice that I sometimes use the term "stitching," and sometimes "sewing." They are not exactly the same, but it's become traditional to use them interchangeably. Sewing is the craft of attaching layers of fabric or other material like leather or sailcloth, together. Stitching is each technically the act of putting a needle through a fabric, looping the thread around itself, and going through the fabric again. All the stitches are the components that go into sewing.

What I normally do is hold the spool in front of me, grasp the free end of thread, pull it out to my side to one arm-length (a gentle, elbow-bent arm's length, not a totally, tautly stretched out one.) Then I pull a second arm-length, maybe not quite so long. When you've done that, cut the thread at the edge of where it's coming off the spool. Good job!

Okay, ready to thread the needle? I've read where people say you need to use a needle threader and some wax. I haven't mentioned either of these things in your equipment basket because I think they are totally unnecessary.

You use the needle threader by pushing the little triangle of wire filament through the eye of the needle, then put the thread through that and pull it back again so the thread goes into the needle's eye as the wire triangle comes out. But that little wire triangle is so thin that it breaks after only a few uses. Although they are inexpensive, it can add up when you have to keep replacing them. And about the wax, I don't even know what kind of wax they'd be talking about, but I really don't want to have to buy another thing and I also can't really picture how they get the wax on the thread. Swipe a piece of wax over the thread? One swipe? Two? Who knows?

Basically, if you have your glasses on and you have a good sewing light, you don't need the needle threader—it's just an extra step that you are paying for over and over by buying a needle threader in the first place and then replacing it every time it breaks. I have a much better way. It's the old-fashioned way my Grandma did it and it works every time. Just hold the needle up to the light and follow my grandma's advice: thread it fine.

Put the damp end of the thread through the eye of the needle
and pull it a little ways out the other side.

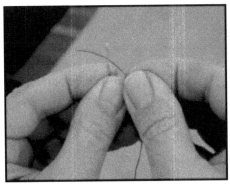

Lick that forefinger again like you did with the iron (and make sure you haven't been eating chocolate cake or red berries.) Now grasp one end of the thread with that damp forefinger and its adjoining thumb. That will dampen the thread end just enough to make it stick out straight—that makes it nice and easy for you to zip it right in there into the eye.

TIP After you've been using your thread a bit and you sometimes have to have to thread your needle again, you might find that there's one or two little fuzzy strands sticking off the end of the thread. That piece of the thread will never go through the eye of the needle because it's gotten too soft. So just snip the edge of the thread so that little strands are gone. Then go back to the finger-lickin' part of the process.

When you've got the thread through the eye of the needle, pull it through until the two thread ends meet, and make a knot. As a basic rule we always sew with double thread. It makes the stitches much stronger.

Now we're going to stitch on our practice fabric. Yes, we are. We're not going to work on some piece of your good clothing until you have the hang of the stitching. You've waited this long to hand-sew your ailing wardrobe. You can wait a little longer and learn to do it right.

Pick up your prepared (ironed if necessary, folded, creased, and pinned) fabric with your non-dominant hand. I (lefty) hold the fabric with the bottom fold (edge) to my right and the rest of it to my left. I hold the fabric with my right hand and start stitching with my left hand in the direction away from myself.

Here's how to hold the fabric for sewing: put your thumb over the fabric and your ring finger under it, at the part of the fold closest to you, then put your pointer finger over and your middle finger under, about two to three inches further along the fold. If you're right handed, you'll do the opposite.

This is how you hold the fabric for sewing.

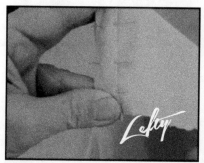
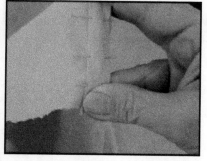

The main point is you want to hold the fabric so that you are sewing away from yourself. (That's not a safety maneuver, it's a comfort thing.)

Hold the fabric in your non-dominant hand as pictured, with your thumb and ring finger at the bottom edge of the fabric (thumb on top of the fold, and ring finger underneath.) About one to two inches higher, grasp the fabric with your pointer finger on top of the fold and your middle finger on the bottom of the fold.

It may feel clumsy at first to hold the fabric in your non-dominant hand, but you'll get the hang of it pretty quickly. This will allow you to use the needle with your dominant hand.

Hold the fabric in your non-dominant hand and use the needle with your dominant hand.

Author's Aside

When I was in high school (back in the old days) I wanted to be a baton twirler for the football games and parades. On the first day of the class I was standing in a row of about four or five girls. The teacher showed us how to hold the baton and slowly twirl it through the fingers of one hand. Then she said, "Diana. I'm sorry, but I'm afraid you're going to have to do it with your right hand if you want to be part of this group." Well, I did want to, so I tried it, and I learned. After a while, I could throw the baton up in the air with my right hand high enough to let it revolve three times around and then catch it again with the same hand when it came back down. That wasn't always successful, of course, but it worked - I did it once in a parade in my home town and got all kinds of applause and cheers! But you know what? I couldn't have done that with my left hand to save my life.

Okay, now back to work. Holding the fabric as we just discussed, stretch your two sets of fingers apart a bit so you're holding the fabric fairly taut. Hold the fabric with these fingers so that the fabric with the outer folded edge is near your palm and the rest of the fabric is lying in your lap or on the arm of your chair. It should be pretty easy to get the hang of holding the fabric like this. And by now you'll be thanking me and yourself for doing the ironing prep work, which makes the fabric a lot easier to control in your hand.

So here we go! Holding the fabric as we've just seen, pick up your needle with the thumb and pointer finger of your dominant hand, holding it about in the middle. First we have to pull the thread through in a way that will not show the knot on the outside of your completed stitching. The way you are holding your fabric now, you are looking at the inside, and the outside is underneath. Remember when we ironed the crease and then folded another little flap to make a smooth edge? Well at the very bottom of the fabric where you are holding it now, you should see where the little flap is. Stick your threaded needle into that flap and pull the thread up toward you. When you've got it all the way through, you're ready to start the regular stitching, and the knot will be caught in that little flap on the edge and no one will ever see it. (Clever, huh?)

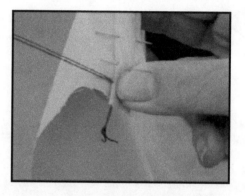

Catch the knot inside the top fold and pull it toward you to the top of the fabric.

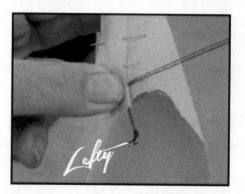

So here's the big moment (drumroll, please.) Holding the fabric in the proper way as shown above, push the needle point gently down through all the layers of fabric, which will be the fold, the tucked-in flap, and the bottom (outside) of the fabric. Now come straight up from underneath with your needle, as close as you can to the down-push, until you can see the tip of the needle come out on the top side again.

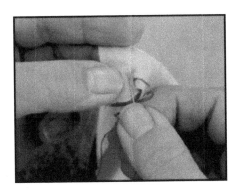

It should look like this.

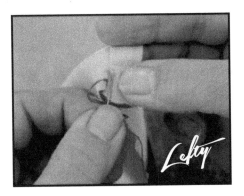

When you see the tip of the needle through the fabric, let go of the bottom of the needle, grasp it again above the fabric, and pull it up through.

Next, you will push it back down through again. Simply put the needle against the fabric directly in line with and about an eighth of an inch away from where you pulled the thread up. Then slide your pointer and middle fingers down a little closer toward the needle so you get a good, taut bit of fabric to push it through.

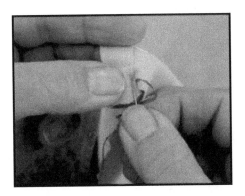

By carefully and evenly pushing the needle down through and back up through your fabric, you are making a neat, smooth, line of stitching.

As you push the needle back in, move your fingers a little closer to it.

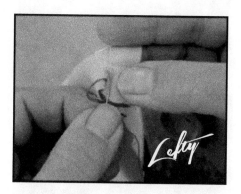

TIP I can see you there, with that look on your face that says "I don't think I can do this. My fingers are too big (or stiff, or clumsy, or whatever)" Don't worry, you'll get it and become fairly quick at making nice, smooth stitches. Just remember EVERYTHING takes practice to get good at it.

Now, as you are pushing the needle down through, gently and steadily, stop as soon as you feel the tip of the needle against your thimbled finger. By doing this, if you put the needle through where you didn't want it (like too far away from the last stitch, or not in a straight line) you can push the needle back up with the thimbled finger out and start that stitch again without leaving a noticeable mark on the fabric.

When you feel the needle with your ring finger and you've got it pretty much where you want it, slide your pointer and middle fingers back up to about where they were before, switch your opposite thumb and forefinger from the end of the needle, go back under the fabric, and then pull the thread all the way back down through it again. This is the most basic of all stitches, called the running stitch.

Don't worry if it takes a while to get the hang of making neat stitches. Practice will make you a smooth and neat stitcher.

As you make these stitches, pull the thread up and down slowly, smoothly and gently so you don't get any knots or tangles in the thread. If you do, you will have to untangle the thread or cut and knot it. You will probably get into the habit, as I have, of touching your ring finger against the fabric underneath as soon as you've pulled the thread all the way through to the top. If you do get a knot or a tangle, you'll feel the little bump and investigate. If it feels smooth, you've done good.

So there you have it. There is no other way to do hand sewing. You can't have tangled and knotted threads all over. Even if you don't care about how it looks, those tangles and knots are actually loose spots in the thread and it will all rip out very quickly and possibly make the original tear or hole bigger than it was. Sorry, but that's the way it is. Once you get the hang of this, it will become one of those things you will do without really thinking about it.

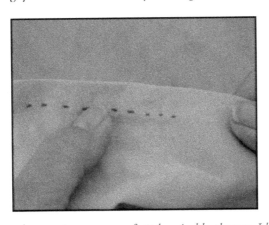

Now you have a nice, neat row of stitches. And by the way, I hope you realize that I used red thread on this salmon-colored fabric so you could see the stitching moves clearly. When you do it, you'll want a color of thread that is the same color as the fabric or close enough that it's unnoticeable.

Now for the last word of instruction on the actual hand sewing. PRAC-TICE! If you don't practice you'll never get the hang of sewing by hand with any kind of ease and neatness. And the meaning of neatness here is that you hardly notice that the stitches are there. Do a little practice sewing while you're watching TV or listening to music. It's actually relaxing. It is! When the line of stitches is pretty straight and each stitch and the space between them is about the same length, then you've got it.

Happy Sewing!

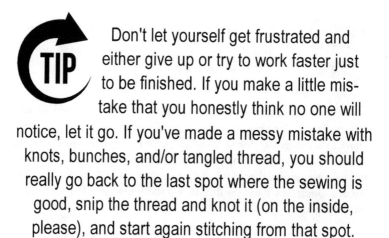 Don't let yourself get frustrated and either give up or try to work faster just to be finished. If you make a little mistake that you honestly think no one will notice, let it go. If you've made a messy mistake with knots, bunches, and/or tangled thread, you should really go back to the last spot where the sewing is good, snip the thread and knot it (on the inside, please), and start again stitching from that spot.

Once you've mastered the basics of how to hold your fabric and how to make a line of neat, basic running stitches, you've got it! There are a million miles you can go in any direction from there, in many types of hand sewing, from repair to decoration. But no matter where you travel in your sewing hobby, just remember: A line of neat running stitches is the foundation for everything else you'd ever like to sew by hand.

THE TAKEAWAY

This chapter is where we actually start our stitching. Let's sum it up for a quick reference.

▶ Hold the fabric in your non-dominant hand and use the needle with your dominant hand.

▶ By carefully and evenly pushing the needle down through and back up through your fabric, you are making a neat, smooth, line of stitching.

▶ Don't worry if it takes a while to get the hang of making neat stitches. Practice will make you a smooth and neat stitcher.

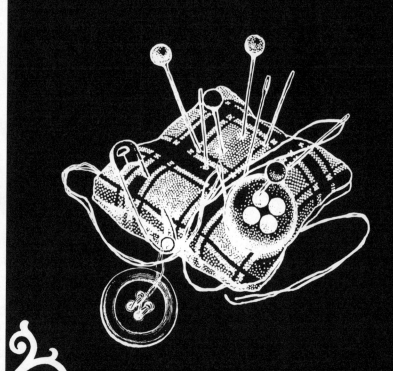

Clothing Repair & Alterations
...You Can Do It!

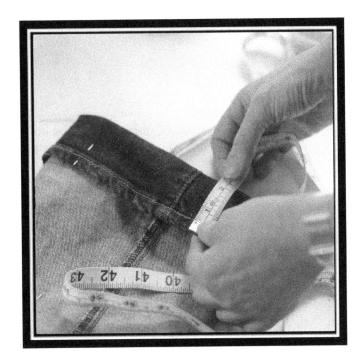

Now that you are mastering that one good line of stitching and can make it fairly unnoticeable from the outside of the fabric, that's all you really need to know to do most of your clothes repair yourself. It will be easier and better looking than you would ever have thought.

There are four things we are going to accomplish in this chapter: sewing up a ripped seam, hemming a pair of pants, shortening sleeves on a shirt, and sewing on buttons so they look good and will stay attached. You may be thinking, "What about repairing or patching holes?" Well, I feel that's a little beyond basic stitching, and there are a number of ways you can do it depending on your needs (and your personal flair.) For that reason I've put repairing and patching holes in the creative household sewing chapter, which is next.

continued...

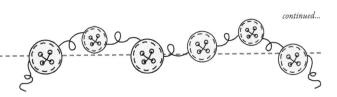

Let's start with one of those ripped seams. Often they are armhole seams, and the long side seams either under the arm or up the back of pants—always somewhere that, when it happens you hope no one will notice, but if you move, everyone will see it.

Repairing a seam is one of the easiest jobs in hand sewing, but you still have to take your time so that it turns out neat. And when we use the term "neat" in hand sewing, we mean virtually unnoticeable from the outside—or as close as we can get to that—just as we did in our practice stitches. You use the same stitch here that you learned last chapter.

 *To sew up a ripped seam, use the plain line of stitching we learned on our practice fabric.*

Whether you've got an armhole seam or under-arm side-seam opened, or if you've split your pants up the back, the repair work is the same. Start by turning the garment inside out. If the whole thing is not totally ripped out, which it rarely is, then you should see the two edges of where the thread broke in between. If there are little pieces of thread still there in the open spot, pick them out (by hand or with your seam ripper) gently until you come to the edges where it's not ripped.

If your piece of clothing is not wrinkled, you really don't need to iron it first, (Of course, if it is wrinkled enough that the ripped seam won't lie flat, then you will have to iron it. But just the ripped seam, not the whole garment.) The easiest and best way to prepare this ripped side-seam for repair is to lay the garment, inside-out, flat on your ironing board with the ripped seam in front of you, in the position it will be in when repaired.

 Have you noticed yet that your ironing board is really convenient for any type of handy work you need to do? Even crafts! It's firm, stable, and at just the right height for you do work on your project while standing up straight and not kinking your back by bending over a table.

Now get out your pin cushion. With the loose ends of the fabric together (right sides are together, because we've turned it inside out) put straight pins in crosswise to where the seam used to be before it ripped out.

Ripped side seam with the pins inserted properly.

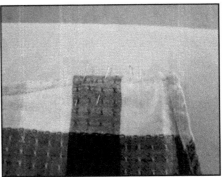

 *For a side-seam, use a straight line of stitching. For the back of pants use a long curve, and for underarm seams, use a shorter, tighter curve.*

Since the seam thread has ripped out, the two edges of the non-ripped part are not secured (knotted.) You don't want to take out more of the seam to get enough thread ends to make a knot in that edge part, because then you will have to do more sewing than you should need to. Instead, go back onto that part that's still sewn for about an inch (no more) and make a few stitches (with your own knotted thread) right on top of where that still-sewn edge is, and that will anchor both the old and new thread ends down.

Most of the time you will be able to see the seam line crease where the old thread was before it ripped out. This will make it much easier to sew the straight curved line of the stitching you need to replace. If you can't see that line you'll have to do it by eye, but with practice you'll get good at it. Just keep your eye on the edge where the stitching begins again. As long as you're heading for that and can visualize your stitches meeting up with that edge you'll be fine.

Now do your stitching just like we did with the practice fabric, and when you get to the other edge, continue on for about an inch of overlap with the old thread and make a few more stitches in the one spot to anchor that side down. As you're going along, make your stitches snug, but not tight enough to bunch up the fabric.

continued...

51

To make your repair work sturdy, you have to do it again. Just start over and re-sew that seam one more time, right on top of the other one, as close as you can get it.

For strength, sew a little over the edges of where the seam is still sewn to anchor both the old and the new thread—and always sew seams twice!

As you are stitching, you will provide more stitches and double the thread to keep the fabric strongly together, and you will make it overlap on any spaces you had between stitches on the first line of sewing. Don't worry about the stitches overlapping. That will basically happen automatically, and that's a good thing, because it will eliminate any gaps in the line of sewing.

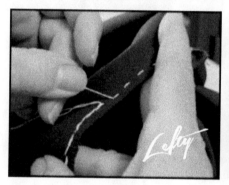

Sew it again, Sam! Double-stitching will allow your repair job to survive repeated wearing and washing.

Now turn your fabric back right-side-out. If you've kept pretty close to the line of where the original seam was, you shouldn't see any thread from the outside. If you see one or two stitches, that would be where you went off your sight line a little bit. If you can see the whole line of stitching, though, that means you were either way off the sight line to the end of the ripped part, or you sewed the stitches much too loose. Of course, if you pull the stitches really tight, the sewing line will get bunchy. Don't over-worry about this. This is one of those bits of correction that you will only have to do maybe once or twice. After that your fingers will naturally get the feel for how loose or tight the stitches should be.

And that's it for repairing seams. It is a little tedious, I know, but well worth the good end result.

Now we're ready to hem some pants, okay? I think pants are very easy, once you know the steps. (I'll bet you thought sewing on buttons was easiest. Wrong, as far as I'm concerned. You can decide later when we talk about sewing on buttons.)

Can I vent for a minute please? I admit I'm getting older and maybe "set in my ways" as they say, but one of the worst things I can picture on people (other than multiple face piercings) is a pair of jeans that are either folded up two or three times into a wide cuff, or a pair of jeans that looks like it fits perfectly except at the bottom, where there is a bunched up wrinkle of jeans floating around the ankle. And usually when that's the case, the end (bottom) part of the jeans is often all tattered from being stepped on and dragged along the floor or ground.

Uh-uh! If you were my kid, or anyone else I know, I'd offer to hem the jeans for you. Once. Then I'd teach you exactly what you are about to learn next.

The absolute first thing you do in hemming a pair of pants or any other hand sewing is—you guessed it (I hope)—**the preparation!** So let's set up the ironing board and iron the way I've already explained to you, okay?

Determine your inseam. This is the first thing you have to learn when hemming pants (well, the second after the iron and ironing board setup.) The inseam is the exact length in inches from the crotch of the pants (the place where there are the four seams that join the two legs and the front and back of the pants) to the bottom edge. Where the bottom edge goes is up to you, somewhat. We all pretty much know, when we look down and see the bottom of our pants and the front of our shoes, what looks good to us. There can be a difference depending on what shoes you wear with these particular pants. I wear my pants so that the end is right about at the bottom of my inside ankle. The expert consensus seems to be just about an inch off the floor when you are wearing shoes.

TIP Mostly for ladies—because you often wear shoes with different height heels, you may have to put on the shoes you would like to wear with those particular pants most of the time, and then stick to the inch-off-the-floor rule. I'd say, basically, if you have enough pairs of different heel-height shoes for this to bo a problom, thon you probably havo onough pairs of slacks to have a pair hemmed right for each height.

All right. So we have the concept of how the pants should look when you stand straight and look down at your feet, or look into a full-length mirror at the sides of your feet.

Now the question is, how do we know how long the pants are when they look good? Well, that's your inseam length, and it's actually pretty easy to determine in one of two ways. One way is pretty easy, and the other is downright simple.

Here's the pretty easy way. Have someone (preferably a loved one) measure from the inside of your leg where it joins your pelvic area, down to the bottom of your inside ankle with your tape measure. That's your inseam, measured to just about one inch off the floor (wearing the heel-height shoes you want to wear with those pants.) You really can't do this yourself, unless you'd want to pin or scotch-tape the tap measure to the bottom of your ankle and work your way up with the tape measure as you stand up. I really don't think that will work well. Either the pins will hurt or the tape will fall off, or you'll bend wrong when you stand up, thus distorting the measurement and possibly hurting your back. So, I would suggest either having a good friend do this for you or instead opt for the downright simple way, as described next.

Get out a pair of your favorite pants that you know you always look good in and make you feel stylin'. Now grasp those pants with the bottom feet holes in your two hands. Put the two inside seams together and then put each outside seam against its inside seam. Now you should be holding the pants with the fingers of each hand at the right and left sides. When you are doing this, you are actually holding the pants sideways, and where your fingers are is the bottom (you're holding them upside down, remember?) of the front and back creases of the pant leg.

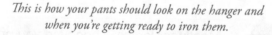

This is how your pants should look on the hanger and when you're getting ready to iron them.

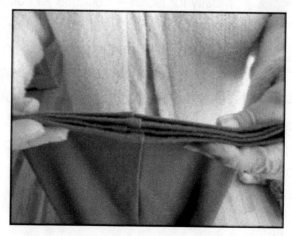

TIP By the way, this is also the way to fold your pants when you hang them up. Whether you put the bottoms on those little clips on some hangers, or you neatly fold the pants half-way over the hanger rod, they will stay fairly neat in the closet until you are ready to wear them.

You then lay the pants on the ironing board with the legs on the board and the torso and waist-band part hanging off the front end of the board. You don't need the iron at the moment, so especially if you're tall—you can get the whole leg onto the ironing board. Next, you lift up the "top" leg of the folded pants and move it out of the way, hanging it off the front of the ironing board along with the torso and waist-band.

Your stylin' pants with the inseam measured.

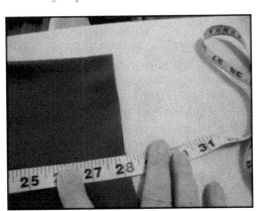

Now you should see on your ironing board the one pant leg with the inside seam up, and you can see from the crossed seam lines where the pants are joined together at the crotch all the way down to the bottom end of the pant leg. Voilà! Before your very eyes, you have the correct length of your personal inseam, as demonstrated by your favorite pants that always make you look and feel good when you wear them! And don't be telling me that you think the rolled up jeans or the bulgy ankle ones with the tattered edges look good on you. Go get the pair that you look good in partly because they're the right length! You know which ones—the pants your mother or wife would make you wear if you were going to see Grandma.

Now all you have to do is get out that measuring tape and see how many inches it is from the crotch (where the four seems join) and the bottom. Then you write down in your sewing basket notebook: "Pants inseam (your name), _ _ inches." Yes, write your name there, even though you already know it. I could say you might want to get a part-time job hemming pants so you want to make sure which measurement is yours. But in fact I'll bet you won't do that. Hey, we're all getting older every day, and the more info you write down when you leave yourself a note, the less the chances of you saying to yourself "What the heck did I write that for?"

So now, you brilliant sewing master, whenever you have to hem your pants from now on, you can just look in your notebook for your own personal inseam measurement, and then skip to step two, as follows.

Put away your inseam-measuring pants. Let's be neat, right? Now, find your too-long pants from wherever you left them, and turn them inside out. Then take these inside-out pants and lay them on the ironing board with one leg lying flat on its outside part and the inseam (the line of sewing that goes up the inside of the leg) on top, and the other leg flipped out of the way (just like when you were measuring your inseam.)

On the ironing board there, these pants should look exactly the same as the model inseam pair. Except for the length, of course, and the fact that they are inside out. Lay the pants on the ironing board in inseam-measuring position, and no matter how long they might be, measure from that crossed joining seam down to the length you wrote in your notebook, and then put a pencil mark at that point. I would say put a short line right beside the correct measurement on the measuring tape—it's going to be on the inside, so no one will ever see it. If you just make a tiny dot, chances are even you won't see it yourself when you need it so don't be afraid to make a noticeable line there about an inch wide with your pencil.

If any of you men have "the belly" and wear your pants below it, take this into consideration when you measure the pants. The reason I'm saying this only to the men is because even though we women get "the belly" too, we still tend to wear our pants around our natural waistline. So what I'm saying, guys, is that the lower you wear your pants, the shorter they are going to have to be. And there's nothing wrong with that—it's just something to keep in mind. If that's the way you wear your pants, then choose a pair you wear like that for your model measurement. The only way you can wear your pants around your waist with a big belly is with suspenders. And that's okay too. Any way you do is fine, as long as it looks neat. I'm just telling you so that you measure them right.

Back to the hemming—by the way, have you figured out yet that the biggest and least easy part of hand sewing is getting the darned thing prepared for the sewing? (Ha! I know I've already said that ten times—I'm just testing to see if you're really reading the whole book!) Maybe that's why I find the actual sewing part relaxing!

So now you have one leg of your to-be-hemmed pants inside out on your ironing board, with a pencil mark at the place where the pants should end after hemming. Put the tip of your index finger against the mark you made. Next, fold the pant leg up to where you feel your finger tip. Right beside your finger (not ON it) iron a crease lightly at the fold—just a little one. Then unfold it and see if your crease is on the pencil mark. Keep re-adjusting the fold until you get it right on the mark. I know it might sound kind of hard to get that crease on the correct spot with the pencil mark, but I have faith in you.

To-be-hemmed pants with pencil mark.

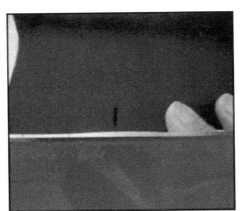

Now, fold the pant leg up all around so it looks even with where it's creased to your mark. But don't crease it all around yet. Get your tape measure, and measure the exact length from the place where you made your crease to the edge of the folded-up part. And I mean exact. If it's one and one-eighth make sure all your measurements are one and one-eighth inches.

*Measure the length from your crease to the edge
of the folded-up pant leg.*

Now, move the pant leg a bit on the ironing board so that the creased part is a little closer to you (two inches at the most.) Measure the next part of the fold that's not creased yet and adjust it until it is exactly the same as the measurement of the creased part, and then crease this new part. Keep moving the pant leg and creasing it an inch or two at a time, and before you know it you'll have a nice sharp, even crease that will eventually be the bottom edge of your neatly hemmed pant leg.

TIP This is one of those times when your reading glasses (or even a pair of magnifying glasses from the dollar store) might come in handy, unless you are under forty years old.

Take a look at the amount of fabric you have turned up for your fold. I am a short person and usually I have to shorten my pants by quite a bit (unless I buy petites, which they don't make for men's pants because the word is not manly, I guess.)

Special Feature

"Clothes Sizes"

For those who've never had the occasion to know clothes sizes, women's slacks come in the same sizes as dress sizes, and then they will be either tall, average, or petite. Men's pant sizes are shown with just two numbers, sometimes without any identification. The first number (if identified it will be W) is the waist measurement, and the second number (L, if identified) is the inseam length.

If you know your correct (dress, for ladies, and waist, for men) and inseam size, you may be able to get away with not doing this pants-hemming thing this time. But that is the best-case scenario. You'll often find the slacks you like best and that are in your price range just don't come in your size. If the dress or waist size is different, don't buy the slacks unless you are prepared to take them to a tailor (expensive!) But for inseam size, you can get the longer ones and hem them. Just don't buy pants that are too short for you. There is not enough fabric in the hem to make them longer.

So let's get back to those to-be-hemmed pants we have lying on the ironing board, patiently awaiting our attention. I think life is much more interesting when we take little side trips. (I'd rather be English Ivy than a telephone pole.) A convenient creased width would be about one and a half inches total—from the crease you've made to the edge of the fabric. This allows you enough fabric to make that fold-over for the finished edge and leave you with a nice, narrow and neatly stitched hem. So what we're going to do is cut off the excess fabric that we don't need.

As I mentioned, I'm quite short, so after I measure, I usually have about three inches folded up on my pant leg. Now just picture this: if I hemmed my pants up that whole three inches, no matter how carefully I did my stitches, there would be a "certain charm" to the look of my 3-inch hemmed pants that would make me put those pants in the back of my closet long enough for them not to make me mad when I throw them out. I know this from personal experience. Please, take my word for it.

//

This next part is not going to be hard (or scary) once you get the hang of it. Just make sure that you understand what I've written before you begin cutting.

WARNING!

//

Here's an easy way to do the cutting, and no laughing without trying it, please. Use your tape measure to measure an inch and a half down from the tip of your left thumb. Conveniently enough, my inch and a half just reaches to the bottom crease of my left knuckle. If your inch and a half doesn't touch a convenient landmark, then you might make a pencil mark on your thumb (it will wash off easily) or maybe put a little bit of scotch (tape, of course) or masking tape at that spot.

This is how I measure and cut off excess fabric—the easy way.

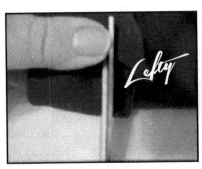
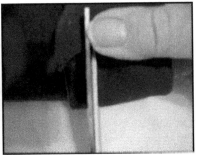

Now, putting your measured thumb marking against the creased edge of the fabric, cut the fabric right above the tip of your thumb toward the open-edge side of the folded up part, parallel to the crease you've made.

Okay, now if you've tried this you are allowed to laugh, but it will be because of the brilliance of this idea. You just move your marked thumb along the hem and cut, instead of having to put down the scissors and pick up the tape measure, do the measuring and mark it, and then put down the tape measure and pick up the scissors again to do the cutting.

Move the pant leg around so the cut part is closer to you and then measure with your marked thumb again, and cut above your thumb tip, parallel to the crease you made.

Here comes the next and last part of this darned pants-hemming preparation (hooray!) Get out your pincushion. Before we get to the actual pinning, here's a cautionary note: Put your pin cushion in a convenient spot near where you are working. This is really quite important. If you put them too near the iron, you could burn your fingers or hand when you reach to get one. If you put the container or pincushion on the higher part of the pant leg and forget to pick it up when you turn the fabric, you'll be sorry! I'm telling you from my own experience of picking up countless little, tiny, hard-to-see straight pins, that this mistake will probably make you quite annoyed with yourself. If you have a table near your ironing board, put the pin container or pincushion there, even though you'll have to reach a little further. If there's no table, pull the pant leg up further to the end of the ironing board, move the iron up closer, and put the pins far enough behind the iron so you don't brush it with your hand or arm when you reach for a pin.

Okay, we're almost done! The next and last thing we're going to do now (hooray again!) is this: Remember how I explained and showed you how to fold over the raw edge of your practice fabric, crease it, and then pin it? That's the same thing we are going to do now.

Just a reminder—you still have the pants inside-out on the ironing board.

Fold the edge (where you have cut it) to the inside, just enough so that you can tuck in that raw edge. Now you have before you the creased edge you've made at the bottom of the pant leg and another soon-to-be-creased fold about an inch and a quarter up from that. (Aha! Remember the inch-and a half measurement for the hem width? Well if you folded just a little bit of the edge over, that was probably about a quarter-inch, leaving you an inch and a quarter for the actual hem. Are we brilliant or what?)

You remember this!

Holding that folded part down with your thumb and middle finger, with your index finger held up out of harm's way, use your iron to crease the fold just an inch or two, insert a straight pin perpendicular to the crease, and then move your pant leg a bit and repeat. This is just the same as we did on the practice fabric.

WARNING! If you do drop any straight pins while you are working – even if it's just one – stop everything and pick it up. Put the iron on its end, off the fabric, and search for that pin, especially if you have little kids or pets in your house. Don't take any chances that you or anyone else will find a pin the hard way!

Now look at what you've got there in front of you: a pant leg shortened to your own personal inseam length, folded, creased, pinned, and ready to sew! Ta-Dah!

Well, except for the fact that you also need to prepare the other pant leg before you actually start sewing. That's life. Take my advice and pin up the other leg now. If you start hemming with only the one leg done and then have to GO back to prepare the other leg, you'll wish you had done them both first. Trust me. Besides, assuming you are only hemming one pair of pants in this sewing session you can put away the iron (emptied of water and cooled off), ironing board, scissors, and tape measure. And another thing (as my mother often used to say) once you get the whole preparation done and your equipment put back where it's supposed to be, then it's time for you to turn on that music or TV, sit in your comfortable chair, and relax as you are hemming your pants.

TIP I would suggest that you do not plan to hem any pants just before you need to wear them. Do it on a day when you don't have a hectic schedule. The preparation part does take almost an hour and the hemming probably another half-hour or hour. By scheduling it this way, if you accidentally take a nap while you are sitting there hemming and relaxing it won't mess up your whole day.

Author's Aside

Please don't get overwhelmed by the amount of work that seems to be involved here. It's really not so bad. You'll probably have both pant legs prepared in much less time than it took me to explain and show it step by step.

So now we're ready to start hemming those pants. But wait a minute —what's the difference between sewing and hemming? Sewing is making a line of stitches for getting two or more layers of fabric attached to each other. Hemming can be done with a straight line of stitches, but something called a hem stitch is used in two other instances as well: One is when you are sewing the edge of a piece of fabric by turning over the raw edge to protect it from damage, and making it into a nice finished edge (like maybe on a table cloth or napkin.) Hemming is also used to make something shorter, where you are doing exactly the same thing as stitching the raw edge, but you make the fold as wide you need it to be in order to make the fabric shorter. Lots of things get hemmed, like pants, skirts, sleeves, curtains, or anything else you need to make shorter.

Shop Talk...

Hem Stitch, noun. This is stitching with a little different technique from straight stitching. It allows us to do two things. One is to convert a raw edge into a finished edge to protect the ends of the fabric, and the other is to make your fabric (or piece of clothing) shorter.

Before we actually get to the hemming itself, there is something else you have to do first. It's a sitting-in-the-chair-with-the-music/TV-playing-job, so I'm including it with the hemming and not the preparation. This little extra step will make all the difference between have a sort of crumpled look to your hem and having a nice smooth, almost invisible hemline.

Here it is: Take the first pant leg you're going to hem, look for that inside seam (the one that will eventually be on the inside of your leg once you turn the pants right-side-out again.) Take out a pin on each side of that seam, and put them in your pincushion. Open out the creases in that section so that you can hold onto the end in our thumb/ring finger and pointer/middle finger maneuver. Don't worry—you've made such a nice crease there that you won't lose the spot when you fold it up again.

Unpin and unfold an inch on each side of the seam,
holding it like you're about to sew it.

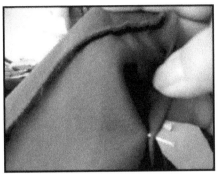

Now, just where the seam and the crease cross each other, take your threaded needle and sew a few times across that spot. Stitch from one side of the seam to the other, right close to its edges. Repeat this maybe four or five times and you'll have a nice, strong stitch point at the bottom crease of your hem.

Stitch(es) sewn across the seam at the hem crease.

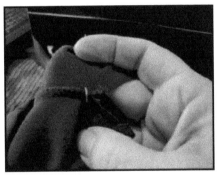

Now might be one of those times you will be glad you made that pusher I told you about. You may be stitching through heavy denim if you're hemming jeans. If you are, you'll be glad to push the needle down and up with the pusher instead of your fingertip.

So now we have a little place where the seam is stitched across at the fold line. Stretch the seam apart as much as you can with your hand, and you should see some of the threads in the seam.

Now take your trusty seam ripper and gently take out that thread. It doesn't matter where you start, as longs as it's BETWEEN that cross stitch you made and the original bottom of the pant leg (before folding.) Put the point of the ripper under one stitch and wiggle it against the thread and the stitch will rip. Do that all the way from the place where you sewed those stitches across the seam, to the original bottom edge of the leg. After that first stitch opens, you may be able to do a few at a time. Just make sure you don't try to rip so many at once that it pulls up and rips the fabric. Aha! Now you know why we did the cross-seam stitches, right? If you take out those stitches down to that spot, your across-the-seam stitches will anchor the rest of the seam that you're not ripping, and keep the thread from unraveling any higher up the pant leg, which we don't want.

Shop Talk...

Ravel/Unravel, noun. These are two words that mean the same thing: the threads at the end of a piece of fabric are coming loose from the way they were woven together. If not protected, the whole fabric could ravel/unravel into separate loose threads.

Also, the thread you are trying to take out will probably be breaking into little pieces instead of coming out all in one piece. That's perfectly okay. When you've got all the stitches ripped, just go back and take the little fuzzies of thread off with your fingers and throw them in the waste basket that I hope you have beside you.

By the way, men's and women's pants often have two lines of stitching at the seams (for extra strength—especially in jeans.) If yours are double-seamed, you'll have to take both of them out.

I know, I know. You want to know why we did that opening of the seam. When I tell you, you'll be so happy to know just how clever a pants hemmer you are. Put the bottom of the pant leg on your lap so that you see that inside seam you just ripped on top, and you can see the still-intact seam under it, through the gap. Gap? Yes. You noticed that those two sides of the seam you just ripped don't meet, right? From where you opened that part to the edge of the fabric it widens out like a V. That is because pants are made to taper out along the leg-length so that the bottom edge is just a little bit wider than the top of the pant leg. It's such a little bit that you probably wouldn't notice it if you hadn't ripped out those few stitches. Designers make that slight taper to make the pants look better along the leg line.

Now fold the fabric back up according to your creases, and put a straight pin back into the hem on each side of the seam where you took it out before you opened that part of the seam. Notice that the edges don't quite meet, due to the V-notch you just made.

The reason we've ripped that bit out and made the V-shaped opening is because of the tapering of the pants we just talked about. If you start

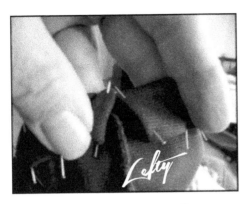 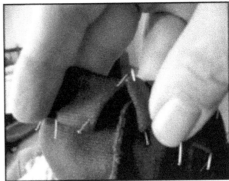

Proper seam edge meeting

hemming at the inseam and you haven't made that V, you will have an extra bulge of fabric when you get back around to your starting point. By making the V, we've allowed a little extra length for the taper. When you get to the end of your sewing on that pant leg, back around to the inseam again, the edges won't quite meet, as we said. This won't show at all because that part will be on the inside. Sometimes you might get a tiny bulge anyway even when you've taken out those stitches. If it does happen, it will be much smaller than it would have been without the V. Just make a teeny-tiny fold and sew it into the hem.

So are you ready to start hemming? (Finally?) Great! Hold the pant leg like you would a regular piece of fabric—like we did in the practice stitching. As

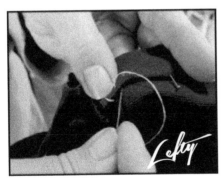 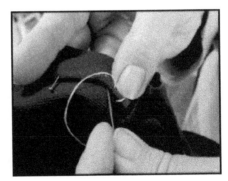

Hold the pant leg for hemming the same way you held the practice fabric.

I mentioned, this hemming is going to be a little different from the other stitching we've done, but it's not at all difficult. Put your threaded needle between the sides of the top fold and pull it up through the crease of the fold (It doesn't have to be exact here, because it's on the inside.)

That puts the thread knot in between (just like we did on our practice fabric) and no one will ever see it. Now, put the needle right back against

 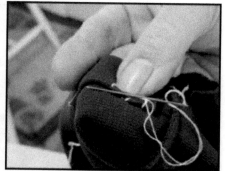

*Pick up as little fabric as possible just above the fold, and then pull
the needle back through and up toward you.*

the fabric just above the fold. With the tip of your needle, dip down and
pick up as little as possible of the fabric and come back up again, pulling
your needle and thread through the fabric and up. When you get really
good at this (and you will), you will be able to pick up only one or two
threads of the fabric.

When you've brought the thread up through, make sure you haven't
pulled it super tight. The stitch should be just tight enough so that it's
holding the (second) crease you made against the outside fabric, just above
the (first and bottom) crease, but not so much that it pulls the second
crease tight. This is very easy to do but pretty hard to explain. We really
need a picture for this one, don't we?

 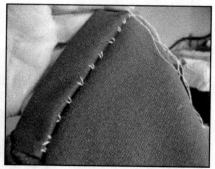

*See the line of stitching as it progresses, holding the fold
against the outside fabric, but not tightly.*

After that just-right stitch, stick the head of the needle horizontally inside the
top of the fold and come out again about a quarter of an inch (at most) away.

Move your fingers over a bit on the pant leg (moving the stitched part
closer to you like we did on the practice fabric) and hold rather firmly with
your thumb on the place where you just put the thread into the fold. Pull

the needle up. Now, right in front of that spot, do that tiny stitch above the fold again, taking as little as possible of the fabric onto the needle. Check again that the stitch is not tight so that it doesn't pull against the fold. Then do the through-the-top-of-the-fold stitch again, and move the stitched part closer to you as you move your fingers further on the fabric. As you're doing this moving of the pant leg, make sure you smooth it out on your lap as you go to keep anything from accidentally bunching up.

TIP Turn the bottom of the pant leg over now, and see if you can see any of the thread from your stitching. Remember that this will be the outside when the pants are turned right-side-out again, and hopefully the stitching will be pretty much unnoticeable from a short distance.

When you do this kind of stitching, the aim is to make a lot of small, almost invisible stitches that will strengthen the line of sewing. That's our aim, but in all likelihood, none of us will ever get it perfect. If you remember to use the closest possible matching thread and do your best to make your stitches small, then, even if we do get a little stitch that we can see here and there, when your pant-legs-to-floor-area is visible to anyone near you, they won't even see them.

As you're hemming along here, take each straight pin out just before you make the stitch, because you are holding the fabric with your fingers and don't need the pin there anymore.

That's it. Just keep going until you get back to where you started! When you do get to the end, just catch up a little bit of fabric from the top of the fold where

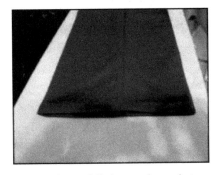

Our beautifully hemmed pant leg!

it won't be seen on the outside, make a knot, and cut your thread. You're done! You can now turn that pant leg back to right-side-out and look at your beautiful work (although you might want to iron the outside of the hemmed pant leg, just to give it a really smooth look. I'm just sayin'.)

Okay, so you're almost done. Well, half done. Now you have to hem the other leg—so here's some Mommishness again: Now you see why you should not leave your pants hemming until you need to wear them! If you plan ahead so you're not in a time-bind, you can stop whenever you want to and pick up the hemming job again later.

By the way, if you think you are proud of yourself now, just wait until you get that other leg done and then wear those pants. You will be feeling wonderful, brilliant, and beautiful or handsome. You did such a great job on those pants. Let's celebrate. Woo hoo!

When hemming a pair of pants, remember that the hem stitch starts just above the top part of the fold and goes into the outer fabric, then comes back up and goes inside the actual fold of the fabric for about a quarter to a half inch in length. We open about an inch of the inseam to allow for the tapering as the pant leg extends downward. Always start hemming at the inseam and go all the way around, so any (tapering) adjustments can be made on the inseam side where they won't show.

Okay, now let's settle down and get back to work. Are you ready to try sleeves? This is going to be a very quick lesson, because you hem sleeves exactly the way you hem pants, and you already know how to do that. The only real difference is that you measure your arm inseam from your armpit to where your wrist bends under your thumb. That's it. Do everything else the same as you did for the pants, and you'll have nicely hemmed (shortened) sleeves.

There is only one exception to the sleeves hemming, and that is when there are cuffs like on dress shirts or blouses. If you want to try these, they are not really hard, but it's very exacting work. You use your seam ripper to carefully take out the stitches on the top edge of the cuff.

Pull out any fuzzy bits of thread and then pin the cuff back onto the sleeve a little higher up so that the length of the sleeve from the armpit seam to the bottom of the cuff is equal to the length of your arm inseam.

Don't forget to jot down your arm inseam length in your notebook (with your name.) No sense in having to do the arm inseam measuring job again next time.

Now, with the cuff pinned to the sleeve, make the tiniest stitches you can. These will not be our hem stitches that we just did for the pants, but instead the first up and down (running) stitches you learned with our practice fabric. Also, use the closest color of thread as you can to the shirt color. And that's all there is to that.

There are two differences when hemming a sleeve instead of a pant leg: The inseam is measured from the armpit to the place where the wrist bends, and if the shirt has cuffs, remove them by taking out the top edge of the stitching, place them higher on the arm fabric, and sew them back on.

Now, shall we sew a few buttons? Well, okay, just one for now. Buttons are really not hard to manage. The first thing to do when you need a new button is look around the bottom of the shirt. Sometimes there will be one or two matching buttons somewhere down there, attached by the good-hearted manufacturer for just such an occasion. If so, you're in luck, and you don't have to search (around the house or store) for a matching button. Remember, you always want to match the button as closely as possible. Here are some button-matching guidelines:

▶ **If you do have to find your own button, make sure it matches in size as well as design and color.** If the button is bigger, it won't go into the buttonhole. If it's smaller, it won't stay in the buttonhole.

▶ **If you don't have or can't find a button that exactly matches the others in looks and size, you'll have to do double duty.** To really be a good sport, you'll have to take off the bottom button and sew it on where the missing one was. Then, you'll sew an as-close-as-you-can button back on for the bottom button hole, and no one will ever know the difference (unless you walk around with your shirt untucked like a hooligan.)

▶ **When you buy buttons—and they do not have to be expensive—just look them all over until you find what you want.** You'll most likely get them on a card of one to about six buttons. That's why we want to have a button container. Eventually, you will probably have so many buttons that you won't have to go to the store for one very often.

Another bit of good luck for you will be if you can see the two or four little holes where the missing button was sewn on.

When those holes are noticeable, your job will be relatively easy. Since the button has to be lined up correctly to fit into the button hole, seeing the two (or four) holes from the former button will save you having to find the right spot—up and down and side to side—to sew on the new button.

If there are some little fuzzy threads left there in the holes, just pull them off with your fingers. They'll be loose.

If you don't see the holes from the old button, don't fret. We'll take care of that situation together right after we do this one. So let's sew on that button!

TIP If there are two holes in the button, you can make a horizontal or vertical line with your stitches. If there are four holes, then it would be either a cross or an ex. It doesn't matter which way they are sewn on, but make it match the way the other buttons were sewn. It's amazing how the eye can notice something that's different, even when the brain can't figure out what is "off."

Now, we'll learn what's called a button stitch. Having the new button nearby, put your needle and thread under the shirt fabric and pull it up through one of those holes (so the knot will be on the inside of the shirt) until you have at least a couple inches of thread pulled through.

Shop Talk...

Button Stitch, noun. This is a series of simple in-and-out stitches through and over two holes of a button.

It really doesn't matter which thread-hole you start with, but it does matter how you situate your button. If you have two thread holes and you have pulled your needle up through the left-side thread hole, then slip one of the holes in the middle of the button over the needle and let it drift down on the thread to the fabric so that it's on the left side. Same thing when there are four thread holes. Just check whether you are coming up through the left, right, top, or bottom hole, and match that corresponding placement with the button.

So now, with the needle and thread pulled through the fabric and the button lying over the needle through one of its holes, push your needle back down into the opposite hole. Make the thread fairly snug, but not super tight. Repeat this so that you have sewed through each pair of holes about four times. That should make the button sturdy in its spot.

So there we are. All done!—Unless, of course, we didn't have the convenient holes noticeably available from the last button. But don't worry. It's really not hard to figure out the correct placement of the button. Button the shirt (except for the missing one, obviously) and lay it on a flat surface. After smoothing the shirt out flat, take your pencil and make a mark right inside the buttonhole that is missing the button. Put the point of your pencil inside the button hole. The mark will then be on the fabric beneath, the same as where the other buttons are already attached.

Make a pencil mark inside the button hole if you don't see the holes from the old button.

When you unbutton the shirt and get ready to sew on the button, remember that the mark is the whole length of the button hole. Move the button-hole side of the shirt out of the way just a bit. Spread out the area where all the buttons are sewn on. Place the button right in the middle of the pencil mark that you made, so that the placement of the holes in the center of the button looks the same as the other buttons.

Next is the tricky part: Holding the button where you just placed it, put your threaded needle up through one of the holes in the button. Then put the needle down through another hole of the button (in the same manner as the others—horizontal, vertical, cross, or ex) and push it down through the fabric again, leaving the stitched thread just a little loose. Now, carefully lay the button holed side of the shirt over the button side, and see if your new button is in the right place to go through the button hole. If so, bravo!

Here's our thread coming up through one of the holes where the old button was. We're placing the hole of our new button on the needle.

If it's not just right, you don't have to start over from the beginning. Since you made that first stitch a little loose, you can lift the button and ever so gently move the button to where it needs to be. Now you can pull the thread a little more—just firmly enough so that you don't make the button pull back over to the wrong spot. Now sew into the rest of the button holes, and it should be properly placed.

This is how it should look when the button is placed properly.

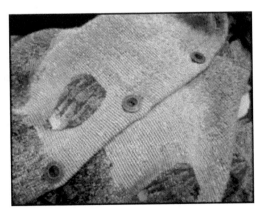

 After sewing the button on (those four stitches through each pair of holes), lift up the edge of the button a bit with your thumb and peek at the thread. If you can lift it more than "a bit" it's on there too loose. If you can't lift it enough to see the thread, then it's on too tight. Somewhere in the middle is ideal. When you've got it right, knot and cut your thread to anchor the new button.

Author's Aside

Here's another anecdote from the olden days. I learned how to sew in high school—yes, Home Economics for girls only. One of the things we had to do was sew a new button on a heavy winter coat (I grew up in New York, so heavy.) What the teacher had us do after we pulled up the thread through the fabric in the right spot was to place a wooden matchstick between the edge of the thread coming out of the fabric and the button. That resulted in the thread on the coat (heavy thread, for heavy buttons and fabric) having just the right amount of tightness/looseness for the button to go through the heavy coat fabric. If you need it, use a matchstick to get a basic idea of how tight or loose the thread should be relative to the density of the fabric. The thicker the fabric, the looser the thread, up to matchstick width.

There is one other thing I have to add here before we are finished with buttons. If you absolutely can't find a button that matches what's on the shirt or blouse, you can buy a set of six buttons on a card and replace all of them. Of course, you can do things however you want, but I really hope I don't meet you somewhere and you have on a shirt with five matching buttons and one that's different in color and/or style, attached to the shirt via nonmatching thread and stitched oppositely to the others.

 *Use replacement buttons and thread that closely match the size and color of the existing buttons. If there are visible holes from the former button, you can use them as guidelines. If there are no hole marks from the old button, button the shirt, lay it flat and make your own marks with a pencil. Stitch over the holes in the button about four times for sturdiness, and in the same pattern as the old ones (horizontal, vertical, cross, or ex.)*

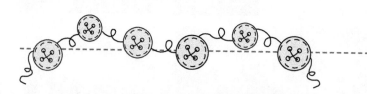

THE TAKEAWAY

▶ To sew up a ripped seam, use the plain line of stitching we learned on our practice fabric.

▶ For a side-seam, use a straight line of stitching. For the back of pants use a long curve, and for underarm seams, use a shorter, tighter curve.

▶ For strength, sew a little over the edges of where the seam is still sewn to anchor both the old and the new thread – and always sew seams twice!

▶ When hemming a pair of pants, remember that the hem stitch starts just above the top part of the fold and goes into the outer fabric, then comes back up and goes inside the actual fold of the fabric for about a quarter to a half inch in length. We open about an inch of the inseam to allow for the tapering as the pant leg extends downward. Always start hemming at the inseam and go all the way around, so any (tapering) adjustments can be made on the inseam side where they won't show.

▶ There are two differences when hemming a sleeve instead of a pant leg: The inseam is measured from the armpit to the place where the wrist bends, and if the shirt has cuffs, remove them by taking out the top edge of the stitching, place them higher on the arm fabric, and sew them back on.

▶ Use replacement buttons and thread that closely match the size and color of the existing buttons. If there are visible holes from the former button, you can use them as guidelines. If there are no hole marks from the old button, button the shirt, lay it flat and make your own marks with a pencil. Stitch over the holes in the button about four times for sturdiness, and in the same pattern as the old ones (horizontal, vertical, cross, or ex.)

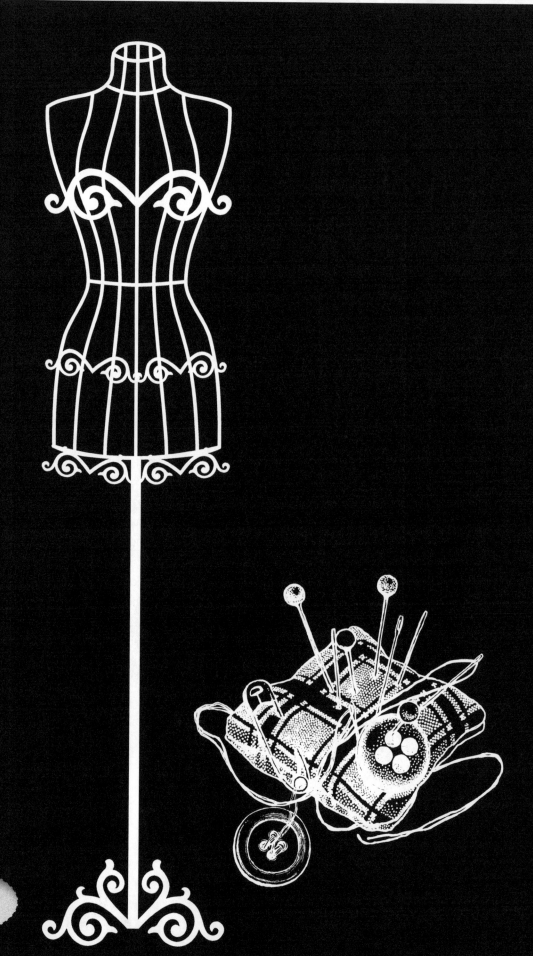

Household Sewing: Creation, Enhancing, Repair, Oh My!

I think this chapter will be a fun one that will give you some ideas, prompt you to think up your own, and suggest some opportunities to be a little unconventional if you want to. And the best thing of all is that you won't have to learn anything new! You've already got all the skills you need. We are not going to get into all the steps involved in actually making creative things like curtains, pillows, etc. (again, that's another whole book.) I'm just mentioning them here briefly to make the point that no matter what type of item you'd like to create, the actual sewing part is the same: You have to make a smooth finished edge, either by preparing the edge of the fabric for a hem stitch, or by putting two pieces of fabric right sides together to make a seam. The only other technique you might want to use in hand sewing is the stitching involved in sewing on a button, and you've got that one too.

continued...

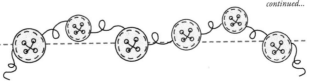

Just as a quick reminder, we've been through seam (regular) stitching, hem stitching, and button stitching. That's it! There's no other kind of stitching you need to know unless you decide to try embroidery, and as I've mentioned before, that's a different subject.

So let's just think a minute and come up with some ideas for creative things we could make. Remember, we are talking about household sewing here—not crafts. This "how to" only describes the actual sewing work. How about sofa pillows? Curtains? Tablecloths and fancy napkins? A lovely throw for your sofa? That's all I can think of for the moment, but I'll bet you can think of a few more. Yes, I heard you..."What about patching holes that we skipped over in the repair chapter?" Well, yes, that too. It is really repair work, but I like to make it creative, as you'll see when we get to that part.

Whether you want to make a curtain, a tablecloth and/or napkins, or a sofa pillow, the actual sewing techniques are all the same things you've already learned in this book.

What you've already learned (and you received a grade of A⁺, by the way, excellent work) is that first you have to prepare the fabric for sewing. That means using the ironing to get rid of major wrinkles, as well as folding, measuring, and creasing folds. Then, pin the fabric with straight pins as you would for either the hem stitch or the seam stitch.

Do keep in mind that whatever we want to prepare and then create, we have to have a proper surface to work on. It would be nice to have a dedicated craft area. Do you have one? I don't. I work in my bedroom. It's comfortable to me, and I can lay everything out on my bed, ready for when I need it. AND, if I get disturbed in process, I just leave the room and shut the door 'til later.

Don't sew in bed if there is a husband, wife, child, pet, or significant other sleeping next to you. If you do get interrupted mid sewing-preparation, don't forget to go back later and clean everything up before night falls and you are so tired that you just want to go to sleep. If you do forget, you'll be mad at yourself. Believe me.

The only thing we haven't talked about in our sewing preparation is how to handle a piece of fabric that is very large, like a tablecloth or curtain. Here's my tried and true advice: Set your ironing board at the edge of the bed, and start by holding one end of your fabric and letting the rest hang down in front of you between your body and the ironing board. It might touch the floor or carpet if it's a large item like a curtain, and that's okay as long as you keep it from getting dirty. Lift the near end (that you are holding) onto your ironing board, and as you prepare each section, move it away from you, toward and then onto the bed.

If the item is wide as well as long, like a large curtain, you can still manage it. Begin as above but only work on the amount of fabric that fits sideways onto the ironing board.

With the bulk of the fabric lying on your bed, start working on the area that will be the bottom edge, furthest away from your dominant hand. You'll have to gently bunch the closer part of the fabric up on the ironing board (without letting it touch up against the hot iron) and then letting it go over the (pointy) edge of the ironing board as it is folded, ironed, and pinned. This might be a bit of a difficult maneuver, but it is a lot better and easier than doing the opposite way—pulling it toward you with all the pinning, etc., already done. So you'll do your preparation work and then move the completed area off the ironing board so that it hangs (gently) off the pointy edge, and start on the next section.

So now we've talked about creative household sewing that really boils down to seam-sewing and hem stitching, no matter what it is you want to make. But what about repairing and patching holes in fabric? And what did I mean about enhancing? I know this would normally be part of our repair sewing but it can also be creative, if you feel like doing the extra bit. Yes, of course I'll explain what I mean!

In my eyes, a hole or jagged tear that got ripped in the fabric of your clothing is something terribly wrong with your garment. On the other hand, a seam that opened, pant legs or sleeves that are too long, missing buttons—these are small things.

While just about everything is fixable, the question is how much time, effort, and/or money you would want to spend on it. That's a question only you can answer, but I'll give you some guidelines to help you decide what to do about that hole in your fabric. For starters, if it's your best suit or dress and you just got it and paid a mint for it, take it to a tailor and get an estimate on having it rewoven. Yes, if it's that expensive that you should get an estimate. Then decide.

I'm sure you know the basic concept of how cloth (fabric) is made. There are a bunch of threads fastened in parallel lines on a loom, then another thread weaves in an out of those lines, first over and under each thread in turn horizontally, and then (without cutting the thread) moving up just above that line of weaving in and out, start another row and do the same. So if there's an actual hole in the fabric of your best suit, the repairer would actually get matching thread and reweave it into the fabric. Since the garment is already made, it's not possible to put the fabric on a loom, so that makes it all the harder to do a neat re-weave. And if there's any kind of pattern to the fabric, that has to be woven in also. You can see why a tailor will most likely charge quite a lot for the service.

If you have a hole or tear in a garment and you can't or don't want to spend the money for the reweave (it may cost more than you spent for the garment in the first place) then you should try to repair it yourself. If what you have to repair is not exactly a round hole with fabric missing, but a tear in the fabric that is not on a seam, you can fix it either by putting the two sides of the tear together, right sides together, and sewing a neat seam stitch to close the tear, or you can sew a patch over the hole. If you feel energetic and creative, you can make an "enhanced patch," which we'll discuss in a little bit.

Basic patching is nothing more than placing a piece of fabric over the hole and sewing it securely with your handy hem stitch to keep the edge of the patch from lifting up. You need to fit the patch to the problem, of course. It should be relatively the same thickness of fabric as the original, and you should make the finished edge of the patch at least one-fourth of an inch bigger around than the hole. Voilà, you're done.

Of course when I mentioned the "finished edge" I assumed you would remember that you have to do the preparing – in this case just the folding-in of the edge and the creasing—to make a finished edge on the patch. Since the patch is small you don't need to pin it or sew the creased edge down. You can just hold it in place as you sew it on. But you knew that. I know you did.

The patching itself is really easy. You sew the patch over the hole with your hem stitch. This is just like you did when you hemmed your pants: Start with your knot on the inside of the fabric and bring your needle up through to the outside. Push it through a bit of the fold, then go back down through the fabric just over the outside edge of the patch, and then pull it back up again through the fabric of the patch.

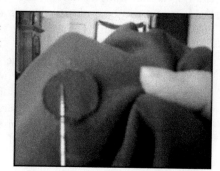

*The patch is secured with
a hem stitch.*

By doing this, you are catching the edges of the patch with your thread, and that will keep it from starting to lift up around the edges or having a raw edge to ravel…or unravel…after you've washed the garment a few times.

KEY POINT *Anything that has a "raw" (unfinished) edge needs to be hemmed to protect it so it can't (un)ravel like an old pair of jeans.*

If you've bought a patch, it already has a finished edge, even though it's not folded in. So just sew it on in the same way you did for the patch you made, except that there's no folded edge to put the needle through. If the patch claims to be an iron-on patch, I'd iron it on, yeah, but then I'd give it a hem stitch around the edge of the patch too for extra strength and non-lifting.

So there you have your basic hole patching. I'd use the patching or seam-stitching method to repair just about any garment that I didn't wear to work in an office or go out for the evening in.

So what about enhanced patching? I remember a pair of jeans I once owned: The first time I wore them, I tore them: on a piece of wire that was sticking out of a

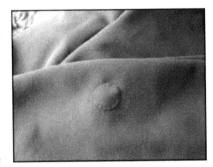

The patch correctly sewn on pants.

fence. It was right on the outside of the knee area. I repaired it by seam-stitching, and then I found a small smiley-face button and sewed it over my repaired rip. I can't tell you how many people remarked on the button on my pants, thought it was cute, and wondered why I thought of doing that. When I said that the button covered up the spot where I'd repaired the tear, I got a lot of compliments on my brilliance and creativity.

Now I realize that you may not want to put anything "cute" on your clothes if you're a guy or a woman who's not into "cute" stuff. But there are all kinds of buttons, if you feel like you'd want to cover up or camouflage your sewing. As a matter of fact,

An "enhanced" repair (the button is sewn on top of the patch.)

there are probably camouflage-styled buttons, and patches too for that matter, as well as the plain and sedately colored and/or decorated variety.

You can be very creative without being cutesy.

The other enhancing method could be the use of an applique instead of a fabric patch. Actually, an applique is a fabric patch, only with a design on it. So again, if the hole or tear is fairly small, you could use an appliqué to cover it.

Sew the applique on in the same way you would sew a patch, securing the edges down onto the fabric.

Being a mom, I'm also quite familiar with repairing holes in kid's clothes. Aside from flowers and bunnies and such there are also camo, skeletons, skull & crossbones, and probably Ninja turtle appliques. It's been so long since I've had to patch my boys' pants that I don't know all of what kind they have now. But go look—I go to Walmart and Jo-Ann Fabrics and other fabric stores, but you have your own options. See what you find. C'mon! It will be fun looking through them.

When fixing a hole or tear in a garment, you can make a patch or buy one, and you can buy appliques in both feminine and masculine styles, but the stitching is the same.

Well, that's about it on the practical side of sewing. You now know the all basics as far as I can tell. You just have to spend some time working at it, on a garment or a piece of fabric that is not critical to being perfect. Maybe do those gardening pants and sweatshirt repairs first. You will get the hang of hand-sewing with a very neat set of stitches before you know it.

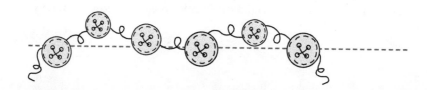

Chapter 6

THE TAKEAWAY

Let's recap our household sewing and repair:

▶ Whether you want to make a curtain, a tablecloth and/or napkins, or a sofa pillow, the actual sewing techniques are all the same things you've already learned in this book.

▶ Anything that has a "raw" (unfinished) edge that has been cut by you or the person in the store that sold you the fabric, needs to be hemmed to protect it so it can't ravel like an old pair of jeans.

▶ When fixing a hole or tear in a garment, you can make a patch or buy one, and you can buy appliqués in both feminine and masculine styles, but the stitching is the same.

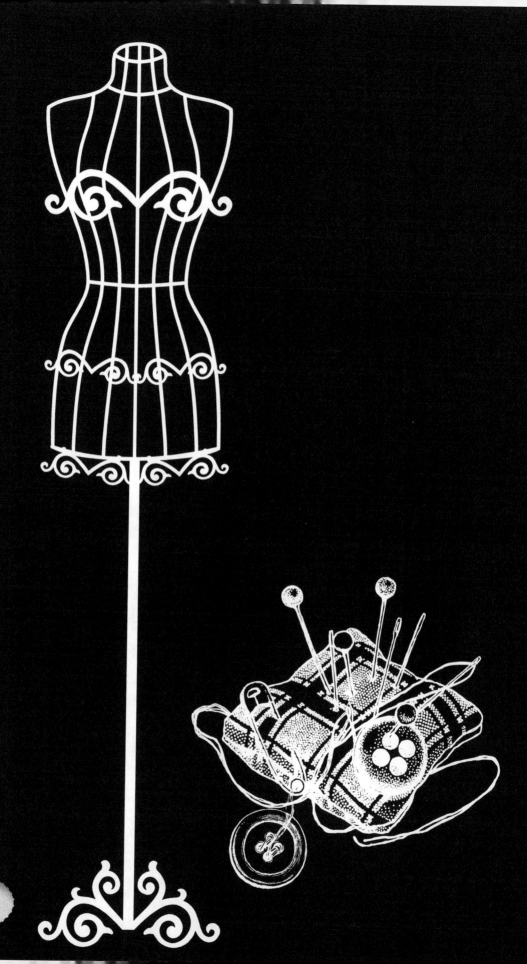

Taking Care of Your Business Wardrobe So You'll Always Look Spiffy at Work!

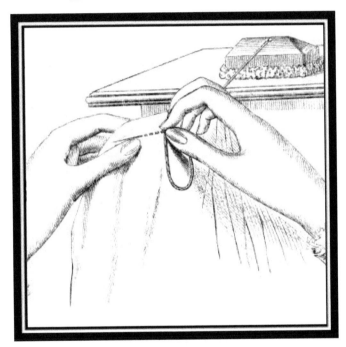

I'm retired, but I still keep the "wardrobe" habits I started when I was working. I always did office work, and when I started—back in the 60's—everyone dressed rather formally for work. Men wore suits and ties and women wore dresses or skirted suits.

Well, as you know those days are gone. Unless you're having a special business event or meeting, things have gotten pretty casual. I guess it started with Casual Fridays, and I can't figure out why someone would come up with that. I mean, you still have to get up, showered, and groomed. What's the big thing about putting on a different kind of clothes one day a week? I also think Casual Fridays started something that evolved way off the original in-

continued...

tent (whatever that might have been.) In some offices, Casual Fridays became "This is my casual look, when I wear my designer jeans, my cashmere sweater, and my Ferragamo boots; what are you wearing?" In others it slowly became "I didn't have to do anything this morning but roll out of bed and put on whatever was draped over my chair (or lying on the floor.) No. I don't like either one of those approaches. This is how things get distorted. You might hear "But I did brush my teeth…" Oh, goodie.

Author's Aside

I spent most of my career in publishing and advertising, working with a lot of artists. I love artists – they're brilliant, funny, creative and many other wonderful things. But they can be, well, different. I worked for one agency where there were many, many days I would see people in their honest-to-goodness pajamas. I asked about it one day and got the reply, "Who cares?"

I care! You know what you look like when you have a "casual day" at home. That's when you and/or your significant other wear your pajamas all day or your too big, faded t-shirt and baggy ripped jeans. But not to work, okay?

 *Keep casual wardrobe for casual occasions, and business wardrobe for business occasions.*

Getting back on track with the business wardrobe discussion: I think of "business wardrobe" by the way, as the part of my closet where all the clothes I wear to work are hanging neatly, clean, ironed and organized into "outfits."

I know, I know. Most of you are thinking "That's nice, but who has the money to buy a bunch of separate business clothes and call them a 'wardrobe'"?

Well, I do—for one important reason. I buy my clothes in Thrift Stores! If you are diligent, you can find beautiful and occasionally brand-new clothing at ridiculously low prices. Try it—I'm just saying. It's really worth it every month or two to have a "thrift store day" just to see what's new.

Author's Aside

I started going to thrift stores about ten years ago, and I always got compliments on my clothes at work. A few years back I talked my daughter-in-law and 13 year-old granddaughter into coming with me. Within a month or two, girls at my granddaughter's school were asking her if her family was rich because she had so many nice clothes. She became a convert, and I'll bet you will too, if you are diligent in searching until you find things of good quality.

Thrift stores are an excellent resource to acquire a full business wardrobe without much cost.

In thinking about office attire, I believe the average office is now in the middle between formal and sloppy, and it's just fine to be in the middle. Being at the extreme edge of anything is not usually a good idea. So for business wear, most items of clothing are fine if they fit decently and are in good shape—as in not ripped, stained, wrinkled, etc.,—and if they are reasonably modest.

Okay, so what should you wear to work? Obviously, men would pretty much wear pants and a shirt every day, with ladies thinking of adding skirts or dresses once in a while, but only if you want to. You don't have too many choices in what you actually wear. But—and it's a big but—do you realize that what those pants and shirts look like can actually make a difference in your career path?

Special Feature...

"Mirroring"

Have you ever heard the advice that you should dress for work in the same general style as the people one level above you? There's some psychological explanation for this having to do with "mirroring"—that is, you organize your external appearance around your superiors, helping you identify yourself with them (and them with you.)

First of all, let's talk about your pants. They can basically be jeans or slacks, depending on your company guidelines and your own preference. But they should not look like you've been wearing them for three days, should not have holes, and they should fit you properly. That is, not so tight that people can see the shape of your thighs and calves (that goes for men and women, but mostly women) and not so loose that they are baggy (same as above, but reverse it.) The bottom of the pants should not drag on the ground (remember our hemming lesson?) Simply put, the pants should look like they are clean, not falling apart, and well-fit. Ideally, they should be ironed so that there is a straight crease going down the front and back of each of the pant legs. Yes, you can iron your pants. You can do it. I'll show you how in a few minutes.

Now, for your shirt. Here's some more Mommish advice: Please tuck your shirt in and wear a belt when you go to work. Even if you have a large waistline (i.e., big belly) it still looks better with your shirt tucked in and a belt holding it in (even if it's under the belly on men.) I don't personally think t-shirts belong in a work place unless it is a uniform shirt or an advertising shirt for the company you work for. I don't mean to come off like an old fuddy-duddy but I guess it comes down to my thinking that the person who looks neat and not sloppy is taken more seriously at work.

Other than that, if you really want to wear something comfortable, get a "golf shirt", which is actually just a t-shirt with a collar. That collar makes a big difference. Or of course you could wear a regular shirt/blouse with short or long sleeves with only the top button open (for men—possibly two for women, but definitely no cleavage showing), and that will present an even more professional yet not overly formal look. And yes, you know you should iron the shirt too.

If you go into work wearing a clean, non-wrinkled, and decently fitted shirt and pair of pants, you'll be fine. If there's a reason for anything more during the work day (like winter chill or a meeting) you could wear (or bring and keep at work) a sports jacket or blazer, a good-looking pullover sweater, or for ladies, a lightweight jacket or jacket-looking sweater. Wearing one of these extras will make your outfit look "finished" and thus make you look even more professional.

And shoes, of course! Please don't wear sneakers (or tennies, whichever) at work unless you do a job where you have to walk around the whole office all day long. I know people often prefer sneakers for their commute, especially in the city where you have to walk a ways to the parking lot or bus stop. But really. How hard is it to keep a pair of nice business shoes in your desk drawer and put them on when you get to work?

TIP Here's another suggestion, mostly for ladies. I do not buy expensive shoes for work. I buy my work shoes in the $10.00 range at Walmart. I used to have two pairs of pumps (black and brown) in my desk drawer. At that price, when they started looking at all scruffy, I'd simply replace them with a new $10 pair. (Smart, huh?)

I hope you agree on the above ideas about what to wear to work. Do you need a lot of different clothes to wear to work? Your answer probably depends on whether you are a man or woman. Men need a clean pair of pants and shirt for each work day, and women ideally would like to have enough clothes for two weeks of work so that they can switch off and not be noticeably wearing the same clothes all the time.

All righty then. We've got the style ideas and we've got the (thrift store?) clothes. So now we just have to keep them in good repair (hence our hand sewing skills!) and in a fresh and neat state in your closet (you guessed it—by ironing them.)

I worked once with a woman who always looked striking at work. Really professional but not overdone. I asked her how she could afford dry cleaning on our salary (we did the same job)—she said she didn't. I asked how she got that nice finished look and she told me she simply used an iron and a "piller."

Huh? As it turns out, when your sweaters start getting old they sometimes build up little fuzz balls, called "pills" for whatever reason, and when they start rubbing against things like your desk or your hands, they get discolored and become noticeable on your sweater.

KEY POINT *Using an iron and a de-piller enhances your existing business wardrobe.*

The "piller" she told me about is actually called a de-piller or de-fuzzer and (like scissors) you can get one for a little or a lot of money. Some de-pillers look like little electric shavers, and I guess you shave the pills or fuzz off your sweater. There is also a cheaper version that looks like a little, fine-toothed comb. You use the de-piller to get those pills off of the sweater and keep it looking like new. The technique is that you comb the sweater and lift those pills up away from the sweater, then cut them off with sharp scissors if they are attached to sweater fuzz. If the pills are attached to an actual string of thread, then leave it alone due to the risk of having the whole sweater unravel while you are wearing it. (Ever see that in a cartoon?)

TIP There is a way to fix those loose strings of thread that sometimes stick out of the outside of your sweater. It's an easy fix, but a bit intricate. Find something fairly (but not extremely) pointy like your computer stylus or a clean toothpick. Push that thread back inside the sweater, and if it's long enough, just tie a knot in it to keep it from going back through to the outside. If the thread is really short but you want to anchor it, you can try taking a threaded needle and catch the end of that short sweater thread with the needle. Then loosely catch a few strands of the inside of the sweater and make that knot—it will keep the sweater thread from working through to the outside again. You're welcome.

And now, on with organizing the "business wardrobe" part of your closet. I used to get my clothes ready for the week all at one time. I'm not the kind of person that can do things like ironing in the morning. Without even getting into a discussion of thinking about what to wear for a nice outfit, getting kids ready for school, gathering up anything I needed to take with me for work or after-work errands, I just never had the oomph to make clothing decisions in the morning. As a matter of fact, I still don't, even minus the job and the kids. But I'll tell you my methods for keeping my business wardrobe in great ready-to-wear condition—in the next chapter.

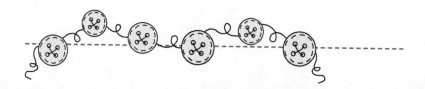

THE TAKEAWAY

▶ Keep casual wardrobe for casual occasions, and business wardrobe for business occasions.

▶ Thrift stores are an excellent resource to acquire a full business wardrobe without much cost.

▶ Using an iron and a de-piller enhances your existing business wardrobe.

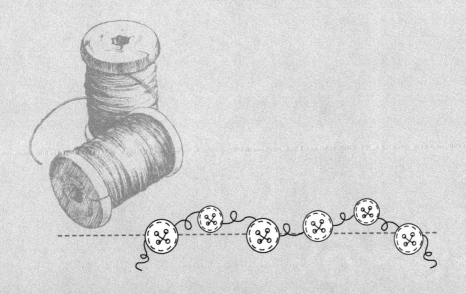

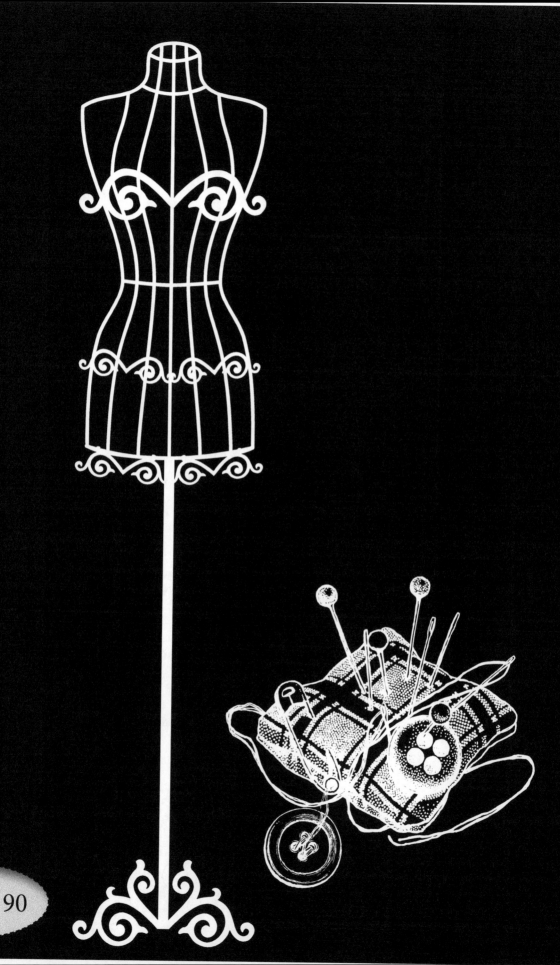

Uh-oh. Back to the Ironing Board.

So by now you know me and my iron. Yes, many of my family members and friends think I'm just plain nutty, but on the other hand, they always say I look nice. For my part, I really like knowing that for the whole week I can just look in my closet and pick an outfit without any on-the-spot work involved. And here's another bonus: While I'm ironing, I use my trusty headset with my phone and make all the social calls that I didn't get time for (or put off) during the week. It makes both the ironing and the phone call less boring. (Yeah multi-tasking!)

I wash and dry my clothes when it is convenient for me. Sometimes I do the whole wardrobe job one day (wash, dry, organize and iron), but usually I split it into the two chores of cleaning and organizing.

continued...

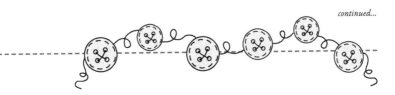

With the clean laundry in a basket, I pick a time (usually on the weekend) and do all my clothes for the next week. I take the clean clothes into my bedroom or living room (depending on who's around to bother me) and lay out all my pants and on the bed or sofa next to each other. Then I go through my clean shirts or blouses and choose one of the "tops" (shirt or blouse) that looks nice and coordinates with each of the pairs of pants (or skirts.) The first time you do this, you may have a couple of pairs of pants and maybe three or four tops left over. If you iron them too, this first time, then you'll always have that many on extra hangers by themselves, either to make a different outfit for next week or in case of some kind of clothes emergency in the morning.

As I iron each paired-up set of pants and shirt, I hang them in a neat row in my closet, and there I am, all set for the next week. In the mornings, I look at the whole batch of them and pick out one hanger, and then check out my extra jackets and sweaters and decide whether I want to wear one that looks nice and coordinates with what I have on the hanger. And there's my professional-looking outfit for the day.

Please note that I'm not trying to say you need an extra sweater or jacket for each work day, especially if you live in a warm climate or it's summertime. But you will keep that spare business jacket or sweater at the office in case of meeting or visitor emergency, right?

 *You can save a lot of time and energy by laying out your wardrobe for the week well ahead of time.*

I mentioned something before about having enough clothes so that you don't wear the same thing every week, right? Well, if you shop at thrift stores, you will eventually have a pretty large wardrobe. I can tell you from experience that there will be co-workers who think you buy a new outfit for every work day.

What? I can barely hear you—you're mumbling. You thought ironing was only to make creases for your sewing repairs? Too bad. If you really don't iron much at all, maybe it's because you think you don't know how.

So here are the guidelines, and you will be surprised at how much of it you already do know (if you've been good and actually went through the hemming section with me, both reading and doing.) Maybe you'll almost like ironing, like I do, or maybe you'll just try it once to humor me. But I guarantee after the first time somebody at work says something about you looking nice, you'll decide the ironing is a worthy chore. Now add to that the good feeling of having made all of your obligatory phone calls for the week, and you'll start off your work week in a great (and good-looking) mood!

Let's start with the jeans or slacks, all right? If you take your pants out of the dryer almost as soon as it stops they may not look wrinkled at all, but they won't have that nice, crisp look that looks very professional at work.

Start off by ironing the waistband of the pants. Yes, it matters. Next, look inside the top part of the pants and find the pocket flaps (if any.) You can't miss them if they're there. They will usually be light-colored cotton fabric that is folded and seamed up. Those are the insides of your pockets, and they are usually all bunched up and wrinkled from the dryer.

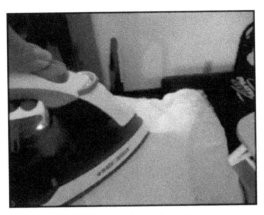

This is how we iron the pockets of our pants.

Lay the first pocket flap out smoothly on the pointed end of the ironing board. With your non-dominant hand, hold the rest of the pants up so the whole thing doesn't slide off the ironing board. Give the flap a few swipes with the iron, and they'll lie nice and flat. And of course, repeat for the other pocket flaps. If you do this part first, the backside and sides of the pants (and you) will look a lot smoother, and as a bonus you won't have trouble every time you get change at the store and try to put it in your pocket.

TIP The reason you iron the pocket flaps before you iron the rest of your pants is so you won't mess up all the ironing work you did on the pants themselves if you do the pocket flaps last.

Now we're ready for the next step. Place the top half of the pants on the board so that you have one side of the front part of the top there in front of you. And make this the side-front with the zipper but not the zipper flap. Iron this side of the pants-front, making sure your nicely ironed pocket flaps

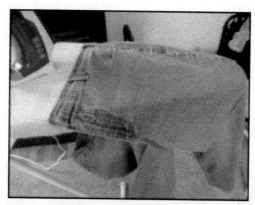

One side of the top part of the pants,
ready for ironing.

are laid out smoothly underneath. Then before you're done with this, iron the inside flap that the zipper is sewn onto.

Now move the pants front toward you so that you have the other side of the front right before you, and iron that part. Finally, move the pants front so that the fly is in the middle of the board. Zip the zipper and then iron the fly-front flat. And there you are with the front nicely ironed. Now move the pants around so that you can iron each side of the back in turn (remembering to smooth out the ironed pocket flaps underneath, if any.)

Now we're ready for the legs. Putting the pant legs on the ironing board for ironing is pretty much the same as we did for hemming. Grasp the pant legs together, upside down so that you are holding them at the bottom of the legs with the inseams together and the "outseams" on the outsides (remember that picture?) That shows you where the creases should be—the ends of where you are holding your pants, which will be the front and back of the legs, actually half-way between the inseam and outseam on each leg.

Lay the pants on the ironing board that way—the way you are holding them and with the bottoms of the legs toward your dominant hand. Iron the upper side of the top leg part first, smoothing out any wrinkles with your hand and then making the creases on the edges.

Next, you will (gently) flip back the top leg and iron the top part of the other leg that is still lying on the ironing board. If you have wrinkles or bulges on that part, smooth them out with your hand, and then iron that nice, crisp crease on each side.

Now, put that flipped-out pant leg back on top of the one you just ironed. Take hold of the pants, one hand on the bottoms of both legs and the other hand on the waistband, and flip the whole thing over so that the leg that was

Iron the different areas of a pair of pants in this order:

1. Waistband
2. Pocket flaps
3. Front of pants
4. Inside zipper flap
5. Fly-front flap
6. Pant legs

underneath is now on top. Repeat that whole leg-ironing procedure so that you will have ironed each side of both legs.

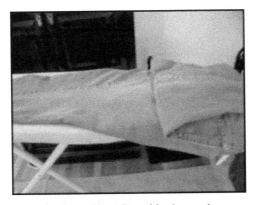

Pants with top flipped back in order to iron the bottom leg.

TIP If you are tall and can't get the entire pant leg on the board, I suggest ironing the bottom part of the leg up to where you would think the knee would be, and then gently (without re-wrinkling) fold that part up and pull the pant leg toward the iron so that you can get to the top part of the leg to iron it.

When you get both legs done and checked for smoothness and no accidental creases where you didn't want them, take the pants again by the ends of the pant legs (upside down) and hang them on a hanger with the two clips holding onto the bottom of the (upside down) pants (or folded neatly over the hanger rod if it doesn't have clips.

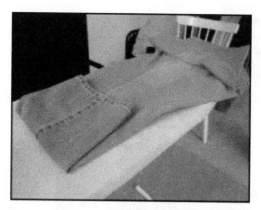

*Pant leg folded so that you can reach the top
if it to iron (if you're that tall.)*

Okay, so now for the shirt/blouse. It's not hard, so don't fret. First we lay the collar on the ironing board and iron the front of it. Then flip it over and iron the back. Then—one of those finishing touches—flip it back to the front again and see if there are any creases that got into the collar while you were ironing the back. If so, iron them out. The reason creases might appear there is because there are two layers of fabric seamed together there. You have to be sure to iron those joined places smoothly to avoid this type of accidental crease.

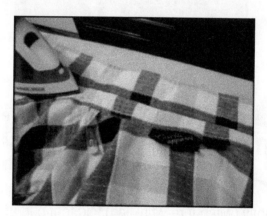

Iron the collar first.

Next, we'll do the sleeves. If there are cuffs, iron them just like you did the collar—front (outside) back (inside) and then front again. Next, pick up one sleeve by the shoulder seam and the end of the sleeve, and lay it on the ironing board. Smooth it down so that the underarm seam is toward you, and on the opposite side there should be a slight natural fold at the outer part of the sleeve. We're going to iron the sleeve from the shoulder seam down to the bottom edge (or the top of the cuff), and then iron the other side.

*Make sure the sleeve is flat on
the ironing board.*

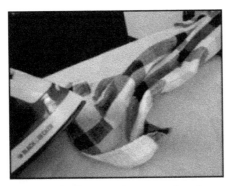

*Lay the sleeve on the ironing board
and iron the cuff first.*

If you want the crease, just iron the sleeve flat after you have it positioned with the underarm seam toward you. If you don't, iron close to the fold opposite the seam, but not over the edge.

Now, of course, you will do the same for the other sleeve. And after that, you'll iron the back of the shirt or blouse. Some shirts will have a cross-ways seam an inch or two below the shoulder line that attaches the back shoulder area to the rest of the bottom of the shirt-back. If this is the case with the shirt you are ironing, don't worry. Just make sure that as you iron that top part you don't put creases in that top part. The idea is the same idea as with collars and cuffs.

*Iron the spaces between the buttons
to smooth them out.*

*Here's the back of our shirt,
positioned for ironing.*

The next part is to iron the front side of the shirt where the buttons are sewn on. First, carefully iron between the buttons to smooth out that strip of fabric where they are sewn on. (Again, it's two layers of fabric like the collar, cuffs, and that possible shoulder part at the top of the back.) Then you'll iron the rest of that half of the front.

Next we'll move to the other side of the front, where the button holes are. We'll iron this side in exactly the same way we did the button side, but it will be slightly easier because you don't have to go around the buttons.

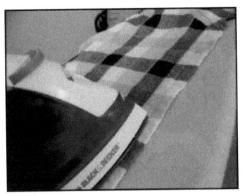

Iron the buttonhole side of the shirt the same way as you did the other.

Iron the different areas of a shirt or blouse in this order:

1. Collar
2. Cuffs
3. Sleeves
4. Back
5. Button Strips on Front
6. Front

That's it! Hooray! You're done! Now all you have to do is put that shirt on the hanger with the pants you paired it up with, and hang the outfit in your closet to wait there cleanly, neatly, and quietly until you want to wear it.

No, no. I didn't forget about ironing dresses and skirts. I just saved them for last because they are very easy (maybe not quick, but easy.)

If you have a dress, iron the top of it just like you would a shirt—collar, cuffs (if any), sleeves, back and then front sides.

Finally, the skirt of a dress and a skirt by itself will be ironed just the same, and it will be very easy. For a skirt by itself, you'll iron the waistband first, just like you did on the pants. Then (for both skirt and bottom of dress), lay the skirt part on the ironing board with the bottom toward your dominant hand, and iron up and down, moving the skirt slightly toward or away from you (whichever is the most comfortable) as you iron. Zip. You're done. (If it's a full skirt, it's going to be zip, zip...and maybe a few more zips, and then you're done.)

TIP If your skirt is either very long or very full, you may have to bunch up the bottom of the skirt part toward your dominant hand so that you can get the top part onto the ironing board. If that's the case, do that top part first and then let it hang neatly off the ironing board while you do the bottom part.

So how do you feel now, you person with all your work clothes for next week lined up in your closet waiting for you to decide which one to wear each day? (Did I hear "pick me! Pick me!" coming from behind your closet door?)

THE TAKEAWAY

We've covered a lot in this chapter about your business wardrobe, but it really boils down to a logical progression through the task:

▶ You can save a lot of time and energy by laying out your wardrobe for the week well ahead of time.

▶ Iron the different areas of a pair of pants in this order:

1. Waistband
2. Pocket flaps
3. Front of pants
4. Inside zipper flap
5. Fly-front flap
6. Pant legs

▶ Iron the different areas of a shirt in this order:

1. Collar
2. Cuffs
3. Sleeves
4. Back

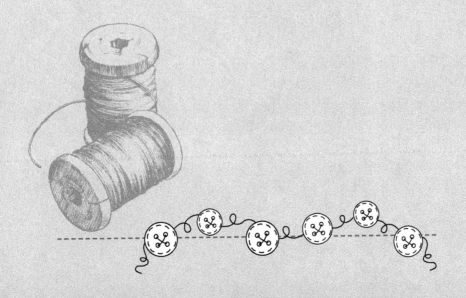

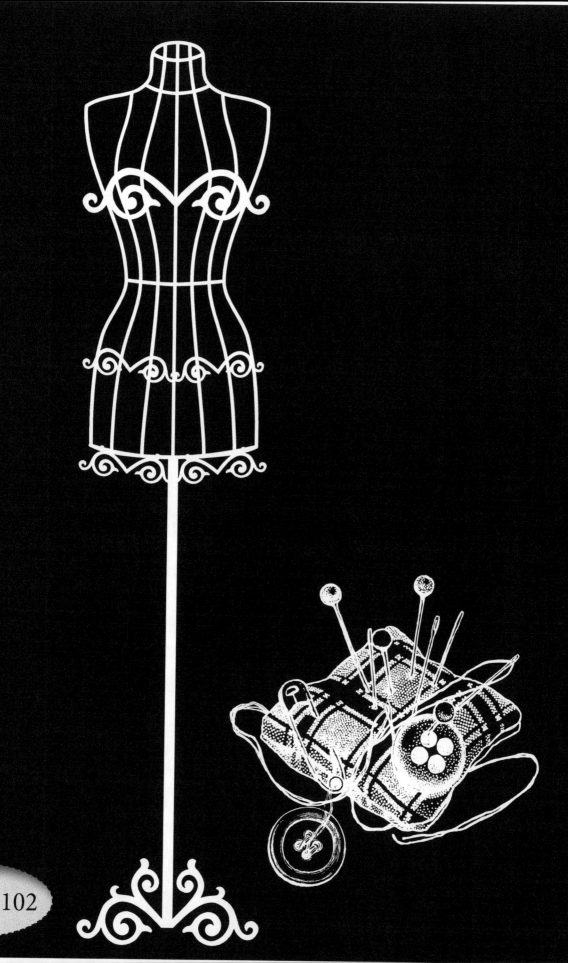

Needlework Art:
A Whole Separate Book.

Remember a little earlier that we talked about hand sewing being relaxing? Well it is—to me and to many other people. If you do find hand sewing a pleasant pastime that's a break from your daily routine, you might try some embroidery. As I've mentioned already, the art of embroidery is not really difficult, but it is very exacting. Some folks think it's a tedious hobby, but to me and to a lot of other people, it's relaxing.

Embroidery is a totally different type of hand sewing from clothes repair, and it's one I'd be glad to give you some help with, but it's another whole book in itself. I just want to say at this point is that it's pleasant to do embroidery and listen to music (which I love) or of course watch TV (which I don't.) But when you're working on an embroidering project that you consider a

continued...

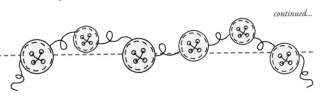

pastime or a hobby, the stitching is almost meditative. When you've got a piece of embroidery completed and properly framed, you'll get a feeling of pride every time you see that piece of needlework art hanging on yours or a loved-one's wall.

 *Sewing can either be simple repair work or an intricate embroidery project that results in a truly artistic picture.*

Yes, needlework is art, and this is the way I categorize it:

- **It can be precious**, as in a child's first attempt at embroidery. And as tangled, dirty, ripped and/or wrinkled as it may be, you might want to frame it—especially if you're the parent or grandparent of the person who created it.

- **It can be cute**, like a picture for a baby or child's bedroom wall, a crib or child's blanket, baby bibs, etc. This is where you'll see all the bunnies and bears and flowers, etc.

- **It can be sophisticated**, like a monogrammed set of table napkins, a beautifully embroidered tablecloth, a sofa pillow, table runner, and about as many other things as you can think of.

- **It can be fantastic.** It can be a piece of artwork framed on your living room wall that gets praise and comments from everyone who sees them.

I work in the fantastic realm at this point, because that's the area where I can bend the rules a little (now that I know the basics by heart) and I can be creative and change the size and/or add my own twists and changes to the project.

And I do mean project. Most of the things I make now take at least a year to complete, if not more. And then, they're quite expensive to frame—especially if, like me, you enjoy making large pictures. At the end of this chapter I'm going to show you pictures of some of the embroidery art that I have done (some framed and some not.) I'm not fishing for compliments here. I just want you to see what's possible. And, I want to qualify it by saying that I have been doing hand sewing and embroidery literally all my life.

I started embroidering when I was a young child. I have three sisters. Two of us are right-handed and two (including me) are left-handed. I can vaguely remember at some point hovering around my grandmother's chair with my sisters, while Grandma showed us all how to knit. Well, as it turned out, my oldest and youngest sisters learned how to knit (and crochet) beautifully—

everything from blankets to sweaters, socks, hats and mittens with pictures on them and everything. The work they do is beautiful, and knitting and crocheting is definitely another branch of needlework art!

Unfortunately, my second-youngest sister and I just couldn't get the idea of the knitting at all. It took years for me to figure out that because both of us are left-handers, everything my grandmother demonstrated about making the crochet or knit stitch was backwards for us! No wonder! Then I didn't feel so bad. And it's also why I have put so many mirrored pictures in this book—it's for you southpaws!

My lefty sister eventually decided that anything involving a needle and thread wasn't for her. But I wanted to learn how to sit and sew like my other two sisters did. So my grandmother showed me how to embroider. I know I started with what's called "stamped embroidery" which means there's an outline of the picture(s) on the fabric, and you basically just follow the outline with a straight line of stitches or a number of little x-stitches.

I know I started doing that before I was ten years old, and from all the other things I've said about myself, you can easily figure out that I've been sewing for a very long time.

I went through the precious stage of embroidery, and I don't at all mean to downgrade it. This "precious stage", as I call it, is the learning experience, and yes, maybe only a loved one would cherish the finished pieces, but that's all right. It's more than all right. It's a necessary stage of learning like anything else. It's the foundation part of the knowledge of embroidery.

Somewhere back a ways in this book I mentioned that there are only about three kinds of stitches that you need for basic hand-sewing. They are the straight stitch, the hem stitch and the button-hole stitch. That is truthfully all you need to keep your wardrobe in good repair. For embroidery, on the other hand, there are a few more types of stitches you can learn and get good at, and then there are many ways you can use those embroidery stitches in different ways to make the finished piece of work look totally different from something else created with the same stitch.

We learned the types of stitches that are needed for repair sewing, but there are many more types of stitches used in embroidery to make a wide variety of effects.

When you are sitting there stitching, it is all sewing, yes. But I like to compare "sewing" with "painting." You can paint the back wall of your living room,

continued...

or you can paint a beautiful picture that is a sophisticated piece of art to hang on that wall. Likewise, you can sew up a torn seam, or you can embroider a beautiful, intricate and sophisticated piece of artwork to hang on your living room wall. There are definitely two sides to each of these crafts, and you can learn one side or both of each—or, of course, none of them if you don't want to.

Here's a picture of one of my embroidery projects!

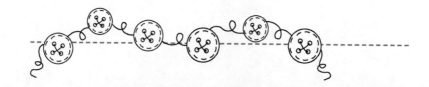

THE TAKEAWAY

Sewing can be very relaxing, so much so that you might want to make it a hobby and take it to the point of being artwork:

▶ Sewing can either be simple repair work or an intricate embroidery project that results in a truly artistic picture.

▶ We learned the types of stitches that are needed for repair sewing, but there are many more types of stitches used in embroidery to make a wide variety of effects.

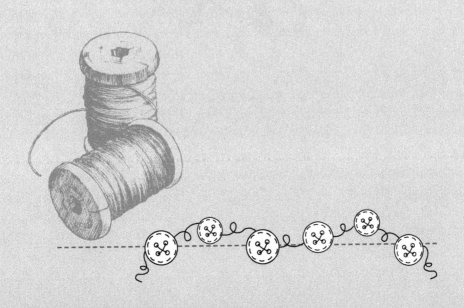

We've covered quite a large area of instruction and practice in the realm of hand sewing. I think it's time for a little break now, first to congratulate yourself for getting through this book (assuming you have done all these activities with me and didn't just sit there and watch me do all the work,) and for learning and practicing how to do that all-important basic running stitch.

Your first efforts may not look perfect, but hey, they will get better. This is the basic learning stitch, and your eyes will eventually learn to gauge a straight line and even spacing. Remember, if you are careful about matching your thread color, little mistakes will hardly be noticeable.

The second thing I'd like you to do now is to think back to the beginning when I was talking about building a foundation for the project you want to complete. Well, that's just what you have done. On the next few pages, you'll find a list of all the Key Points in the book, so you can quickly review whenever you need to.

Thanks for reading!

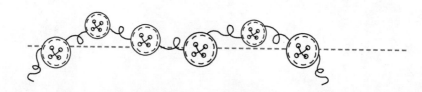

- Hand sewing is one of the earliest human skills. Starting with cavemen trying to protect themselves from cold and injury and evolving all the way to high-fashion design, the actual technique of hand sewing is the same: Two pieces of material/fabric with a needle and thread to attach them to each other.

- In comparison with a sewing machine, the equipment you will need for all your hand sewing will probably cost you around $20.00. If you buy a sewing machine you'll still need all the same equipment plus a few additions.

- We don't need (or even necessarily want) a sewing machine or a professional tailor for clothes hemming or basic repairs. We can keep our wardrobes in tip-top shape with simple and inexpensive hand-sewing.

- Hand sewing can be a very relaxing pastime or hobby.

- By the end of this book you will have two baskets filled with wonderful things (knowledge and equipment) that will help you do quality hand sewing and keep you happy with a serene mind and nice clothes for years to come.

- The equipment you'll need to do a thorough and neat hand-sewing project consists of the following:

  - Needles
  - Thread
  - Tape Measure
  - Straight Pins
  - Pin Cushion
  - Scissors
  - Seam Ripper
  - Thimble and/or Pusher
  - Buttons and a Container to Keep Them In
  - Notepad and Pencil
  - Container for all Your Sewing Equipment
  - Iron and Ironing Board, Stored Separately

- When starting any new job or hobby, you have to learn how to set things up properly before you get into it (and put them away properly when you're done!) There's no other way to end up with a good job.

- If the fabric is very wrinkled, you'll benefit from ironing it before you sew it.

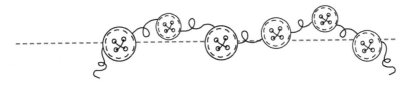

- Hold the fabric in your non-dominant hand and use the needle with your dominant hand.

- By carefully and evenly pushing the needle down through and back up through your fabric, you are making a neat, smooth, line of stitching.

- Don't worry if it takes a while to get the hang of making neat stitches. Practice will make you a smooth and neat stitcher.

- To sew up a ripped seam, use the plain line of stitching we learned on our practice fabric.

- For a side-seam, use a straight line of stitching. For the back of pants use a long curve, and for underarm seams, use a shorter, tighter curve.

- For strength, sew a little over the edges of where the seam is still sewn to anchor both the old and the new thread – and always sew seams twice!

- When hemming a pair of pants, remember that the hem stitch starts just above the top part of the fold and goes into the outer fabric, then comes back up and goes inside the actual fold of the fabric for about a quarter to a half inch in length. We open about an inch of the inseam to allow for the tapering as the pant leg extends downward. Always start hemming at the inseam and go all the way around, so any (tapering) adjustments can be made on the inseam side where they won't show.

- There are two differences when hemming a sleeve instead of a pant leg: The inseam is measured from the armpit to the place where the wrist bends, and if the shirt has cuffs, remove them by taking out the top edge of the stitching, place them higher on the arm fabric, and sew them back on.

- Use replacement buttons and thread that closely match the size and color of the existing buttons. If there are visible holes from the former button, you can use them as guidelines. If there are no hole marks from the old button, button the shirt, lay it flat and make your own marks with a pencil. Stitch over the holes in the button about four times for sturdiness, and in the same pattern as the old ones (horizontal, vertical, cross, or ex.)

- Whether you want to make a curtain, a tablecloth and/or napkins, or a sofa pillow, the actual sewing techniques are all the same things you've already learned in this book.

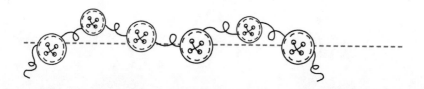

- Anything that has a "raw" (unfinished) edge that has been cut by you or the person in the store that sold you the fabric, needs to be hemmed to protect it so it can't ravel like an old pair of jeans.

- When fixing a hole or tear in a garment, you can make a patch or buy one, and you can buy appliqués in both feminine and masculine styles, but the stitching is the same.

- Keep casual wardrobe for casual occasions, and business wardrobe for business occasions.

- Thrift stores are an excellent resource to acquire a full business wardrobe without much cost.

- Using an iron and a de-piller enhances your existing business wardrobe.

- You can save a lot of time and energy by laying out your wardrobe for the week well ahead of time.

- *Iron the different areas of a pair of pants in this order:*

  1. Waistband
  2. Pocket Flaps
  3. Front of Pants
  4. Inside Zipper Flap
  5. Fly-front Flap
  6. Pant Legs

- *Iron the different areas of a shirt in this order:*

  1. Collar
  2. Cuffs
  3. Sleeves
  4. Back
  5. Button Strips (Front)
  6. Front

- Sewing can either be simple repair work or an intricate embroidery project that results in a truly artistic picture.

- We learned the types of stitches that are needed for repair sewing, but there are many more types of stitches used in embroidery to make a wide variety of effects.

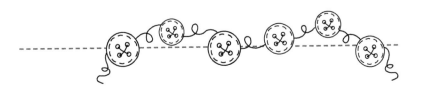

I hope you have found my book easy to understand
and useful, and that you will refer to it often as
you begin to perfect your hand sewing.

Of course, I'm not the only person who is available to help you. In all fairness, I have to list a few other sources that you can also use to learn about hand sewing, and here they are:

- **"18 Hand Sewing Tutorials for Beginners–Hand Stitches Edition"** *http://craftingdelight.net/10-hand-sewing-tutorials-for-beginners-hand-stitches-edition/* (accessed 20142/10/14)

- Detrixe, Sandra. **The Everything Sewing Book: From Threading the Needle to Basting the Hem, All You Need to Alter and Create Beautiful Clothes, Gifts, and Decorations (Everything®)** [Kindle Edition.] Adams Media. 2004

- June, Mimi. **"Learning How To Sew"** *http://www.learninghowtosew.com/* (accessed 2014/9/16)

- Lewis, Sam. **"Hand Sewing for Beginners"** *ehow.com. http://www.ehow.com/video_4767355_hand-sewing-beginners. html* (accessed 2014/8/21)

- **"Sewing Daily: Sewing Made Modern"** *http://www.sewdaily.com/sewing-for-beginners/* (accessed 2014/9/30)

- Smith, Alison and Rupp, Diana. **The Sewing Book: An Encyclopedic Resource of Step-by-Step Techniques** DK Publishing 2009

- Wasinger, Susan. **Sewn by Hand: Two Dozen Projects Stitched with Needle & Thread** Lark Crafts 2011

- Zieman, Nancy. S**ew with Confidence: A Beginner's Guide to Basic Sewing** Krause Publications; 2 edition 2004

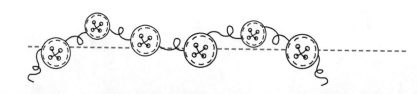

- **Button Stitch**: This is a series of simple in-and-out stitches through and over two holes of a button.

- **Hem Stitch**: This is stitching with a little different technique from straight stitching. It allows us to do two things. One is to convert a raw edge into a finished edge to protect the ends of the fabric, and the other is to make your fabric (or piece of clothing) shorter.

- **Ravel/Unravel**: These are two words that mean the same thing: the threads at the end of a piece of fabric are coming loose from the way they were woven together. If not protected, the whole fabric could ravel/unravel into separate loose threads.

- **Seam Stitch**: This is the straight line of stitching that you would do to attach two or more layers of fabric together.

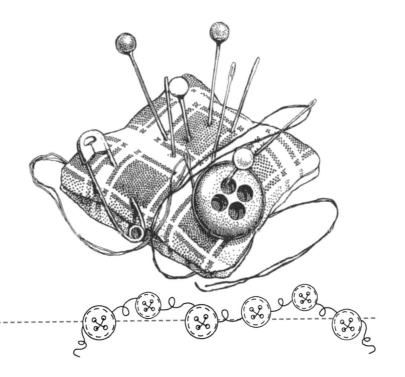

CPSIA information can be obtained
at www.ICGtesting.com
Printed in the USA
BVHW01s2006140818
524340BV00055B/686/P